THE ART OF AI

How Technology Affects Creativity

Harry J. Smith

CONTENTS

Title Page

Copyright

Introduction

Chapter 1: Artificial Intelligence and Human Creativity.   1

Chapter 2: The Basics of Creative AI.   9

Chapter 3: AI in Music   18

Chapter 4: AI in Visual Art   26

Chapter 5: AI in Literature.   34

Chapter 6: AI in Film and Entertainment   42

Chapter 7: AI in Fashion   50

Chapter 8: AI in User Experience Design.   59

Chapter 9: The Ethical Challenges of Creative AI.   67

Chapter 10: Beyond Today: The Future of Creative AI   75

Epilogue   83

About The Author   85

INTRODUCTION

Welcome to the fascinating world where artificial intelligence (AI) meets human creativity: an uncharted territory where science and art, the logical and the irrational, come together in surprising harmony. "The Art of AI: How Technology Influences Creativity" will guide you through this maze of possibilities, challenging your preconceptions of what is possible when these two seemingly disparate forces meet.

Have you ever wondered if an algorithm could compose a symphony capable of emotion? Or if a neural network could paint a picture that challenges our understanding of art? These questions might sound like something out of a science fiction novel, but they are current questions that we are beginning to answer. This book is your map for navigating this new universe.

In Chapter 1, we explore the marriage of AI and human creativity, covering everything from the history of collaboration to the ethical dilemmas that arise when the machine begins to "create." Since understanding the context is crucial, we will give a comprehensive introduction to what AI is, how it began to intertwine its history with that of art, and what the limits and potential of this collaboration are.

From Chapter 2 onward, we get to the heart of the subject, unveiling the basics of creative AI. Generative algorithms, neural networks, deep learning-these terms might seem abstract now, but we promise they will become second nature once you learn how they work and how they can be applied in different areas of creativity.

Because, yes, AI is making inroads into all artistic fields. Imagine music composed with the help of AI that evokes deep emotions, or paintings generated by algorithms that rival the great masters. And that's not all; literature, film and fashion are also experiencing their own revolution thanks to this technology. This book will take you on a journey through these revolutionary applications, showing you concrete examples and success stories.

But we cannot ignore the responsibilities that come with such great power. In Chapter 9, we confront the ethical challenges that accompany creative AI. From copyright attribution to the impact on employment, we explore the dilemmas society faces in using this technology responsibly.

Finally, we invite you to look to the future. Creative AI is a rapidly developing frontier, with innovations emerging at a dizzying pace. What will be its role in the world of art, music, literature and beyond in the coming years? Chapter 10 will attempt to shed some light on these conundrums.

We assure you that you will end this book with a new perspective on creativity and how artificial intelligence is changing the rules of the game. Prepare to be surprised, inspired and, perhaps, a little unsettled, but most of all, prepare to open your mind to a world of endless possibilities.

Welcome to The Art of AI. The future of creativity begins now.

CHAPTER 1: ARTIFICIAL INTELLIGENCE AND HUMAN CREATIVITY.

One of the questions permeating the air of our time, charged with uncertainty and fascination, is: what is artificial intelligence and what role can it play in the increasingly complex fabric of human creativity? It is a question that triggers a deluge of other questions, some technical and some philosophical, all of which are bound to profoundly affect the way we understand the very essence of cognition and innovation.

To begin with, artificial intelligence is a branch of computer science that seeks to build systems capable of performing tasks that, if done by humans, would require the use of intelligence. But beware, this definition is a double-threaded one: while it leads us to compare machine with human, it also forces us to ask what exactly we mean by "intelligence." Is it reasoning? Is it adaptability? Is it the ability to experience and learn from experience? The answer is that intelligence is all of these things, and perhaps more.

Now, let's talk about creativity, that jewel set at the heart of human experience. Creativity is the ability to generate original and valuable ideas, works, and solutions. It is a gift that would seem to belong exclusively to the human domain, where intuition, emotion and connection to a broader cultural heritage play irreplaceable roles. However, here is where the talk gets interesting: artificial intelligence is increasingly involved in the realm of creativity, not as a substitute, but as an amplifier of our capabilities.

Artificial intelligence systems are now being used in fields ranging from art to music, from writing to architectural design. They can analyze huge data sets to identify patterns and trends that would be almost impossible for a single human being to detect. They can generate initial ideas that artists can then shape and refine. In this sense, artificial intelligence acts as a catalyst that can open up new avenues for human inspiration.

But what does this mean for the broader understanding of the relationship between artificial intelligence and human creativity? It means that we must begin to think of these entities not as competing forces, but as complementary components of a larger ecosystem. An ecosystem in which the machine is neither the master nor the slave, but a partner in the process of discovery and creation.

We cannot yet say whether machines will ever be "creative" in the purest and deepest sense of the word, but what we can say is that their presence is already changing the way we create, engage and even think about the concept of creativity. And so, as we continue to navigate these uncharted waters, one thing is certain: the combination of artificial intelligence and human creativity represents one of the most exciting and challenging frontiers of our time.

Let us take a moment to consider artificial intelligence not as a mere computational tool or an effective performer of mechanical tasks, but as a silent companion in the creative journey of the human being. The collaboration between artificial intelligence and human creativity is a story rooted in years of technological and philosophical development. This relationship has become especially relevant in an age when we are constantly seeking new ways to express ourselves and to understand the world around us.

In the early stages of its development, artificial intelligence was seen primarily as a machine for solving complicated mathematical problems. However, as time went on, scientists and thinkers began to ask, "What if AI could do more? What if it could help unlock new levels of creative expression?"

And so began an unusual but fruitful collaboration. Take, for example, the world of digital painting. Here, artificial intelligence can suggest color combinations and patterns that perhaps an artist would never have considered, pushing him beyond the limits of his imagination. Similarly, in musical composition, algorithms can generate harmonic or rhythmic sequences that offer a new space of exploration for the composer. This is not to replace the artist, but to expand his or her repertoire of creative possibilities.

Writing is another domain into which AI is slowly making its foray. Using advanced natural language processing techniques, algorithms can suggest plots, generate dialogue, and even create characters with compelling psychological depth. All this allows writers to focus on more subtle aspects of narrative, such as pacing and tone, while AI handles more mechanical elements.

It is not only in traditional art that AI finds application. Product design, fashion, architecture, and even cooking are beginning to see AI as a partner rather than a tool. Whether suggesting new combinations of materials in the fashion industry or optimizing the distribution of space in a building, AI offers a whole new perspective, based on data and algorithms, that can go hand in hand with human intuition and vision.

However, the relationship between AI and human creativity is not without controversy. There are those who argue that AI, by its very nature, is incapable of true creativity, as it lacks the emotions and subjective experience that are fundamental to the creative act. At the same time, there is a fear that AI may "dehumanize" art, making the human touch superfluous.

Despite these concerns, it is undeniable that we are at a crucial moment in the history of collaboration between artificial intelligence and human creativity. This collaboration has the potential to push the boundaries of art and design into uncharted territories, enriching our understanding of creativity itself. It is a story that has just begun, and its future pages are open to endless possibilities.

One of the most fascinating questions emerging in the dialogue between artificial intelligence and humanity is the challenge to our understanding of creativity. At first glance, creativity seems to be the exclusive domain of humans, an inner landscape so rich and complex that it is inaccessible to an algorithm. However, recent innovations in the field of artificial intelligence are beginning to subvert this notion, presenting case studies that invite deeper reflection.

Take, for example, the field of visual art. A project called "DeepArt" uses convolutional neural networks to 'learn' art styles from famous paintings and apply them to new images. The output is surprising and challenges our understanding of what constitutes a work of art. Could an algorithm, trained to replicate Van Gogh's brushstrokes or Mondrian's geometry, claim any kind of creative agency? The answer to this question may not be a simple "yes" or "no," but rather an invitation to explore what we really mean when we talk about creativity.

In the field of writing, programs like GPT-3 have demonstrated incredible versatility in mimicking the style and structure of human language. While most writers probably do not see these tools as a threat to their profession, they raise intriguing questions about the essence of storytelling and intellectual property. If an algorithm can generate a story or poem that touches the strings of human emotion, how should we confront our previous belief that creativity is the exclusive preserve of the human mind?

In the world of music, artificial intelligence tools such as AIVA or Google's Magenta have composed tracks ranging from classical pieces to electronic music tracks. The output, again, is so compelling that it challenges the traditional barriers between the "created" and the "computed."

These case studies open a Pandora's box of ethical, philosophical and even existential questions. First, there is the question of intellectual property. If an algorithm creates a work of art or composes a symphony, to whom does it really belong? Second, as technology advances, it is inevitable to ask whether there will be a point at which artificial intelligence surpasses humans in terms of creative capabilities. And if so, what kind of implications will this have for our role and sense of identity in the world?

The dialogue between artificial intelligence and human creativity is like a dialogue between mirrors, where each reflection might reveal something new about what it means to be truly 'creative.' Perhaps instead of seeing artificial intelligence as a usurper of our creative domain, we might see it as a complement, an extension that challenges and enriches our understanding of creativity itself.

As we continue to navigate this uncharted territory, it is crucial not only to celebrate our technical achievements but also to ponder the deeper questions these innovations raise. Artificial intelligence and human creativity, far from being conflicting concepts, can actually be fellow travelers in an extraordinary exploration of the infinite potential of expression and imagination.

In the modern era, artificial intelligence (AI) has invaded numerous areas of everyday life, from industrial automation to medical diagnostics. But one of the most fascinating, and at the same time disturbing, questions is the relationship between AI and human creativity. Many wonder whether machines will ever be able to replicate, or even surpass, human creativity. Others question the ethical implications of such a development.

When we talk about creativity, we are referring to the ability to generate original and meaningful ideas, concepts or products. It has always been considered an exclusively human peculiarity, linked to complex cognitive processes and culture. Can machines really compete with humans in this field?

Some recent developments in the field of AI might make us think so. Deep learning algorithms have been trained to compose music, create works of art and write poetry that, at first glance, might appear to be the product of human genius. But can we define "creative" as a machine that does not possess consciousness, emotions or an understanding of the context in which it operates?

This is where ethics comes in. The use of AI in the field of creativity opens a real ethical Pandora's box. If an algorithm creates a work of art or composes a symphony, who owns the copyright? And what happens when AI generates content that is considered offensive or inappropriate? Who is responsible: the machine, the programmer, or the one who provided the data for training?

In addition to legal dilemmas, there is a growing concern about the effect that technology might have on human creativity itself. If we begin to depend too much on AI to generate "creative" content, we run the risk of eroding our own inventive potential. Creativity is linked to our identity, culture and history; delegating this process to machines could have an irrevocable impact on our evolution as a species.

However, we should not necessarily see AI as a threat to human creativity, but rather as a complement. Artists can use AI to explore new expressive frontiers, musicians to experiment with novel sound structures, and writers to play with new narrative forms. AI could also serve as an educational tool, helping people develop their creative skills through imitation and variation.

The intersection of AI and human creativity is a territory rich in potential but also in danger. The ethical responsibility of navigating this complicated landscape falls on all of us: developers, artists, ethicists and society as a whole. We must proceed with caution, carefully weighing the ethical implications of each technological breakthrough, and always remembering that the true essence of creativity lies in the uniqueness and complexity of the human experience.

Artificial Intelligence is a field that has catalyzed the attention of the scientific, corporate and cultural worlds, challenging conventions about what it means to be creative. At first, many saw Artificial Intelligence as simply a tool, a tool to automate tasks. To date, these intelligent machines are not only capable of solving complex equations or managing huge databases; they are beginning to show signs of a kind of creativity, entering domains once thought to be the exclusive preserve of the human mind.

In the art world, for example, machine learning algorithms are now able to generate paintings, musical compositions and even poems. One might ask whether these works are truly 'creative' or simply the result of complex statistical calculations. The question is controversial and stimulates deep reflections on the very essence of creativity. Is it a process that can be decomposed into data and algorithms, or is there an ineffable quid, irreducible to mathematical formulas?

Human creativity has its own complexity, an interweaving of experiences, emotions and knowledge that eludes a simple computational approach. Humans draw from a mosaic of cultural influences, social interactions and personal insights to create something new and unique. In comparison, Artificial Intelligence lacks this depth and variety of experience; it is confined to the data it has been given and the algorithms that govern it.

But the future is open to fascinating possibilities. As technology evolves, a new class of AI systems equipped with a form of 'computational imagination' is on the horizon. These are algorithms that can 'imagine' future scenarios, form hypotheses or generate original ideas from available data. A symbiotic collaboration between man and machine could arise, in which Artificial Intelligence acts as an amplifier of our creative abilities rather than a substitute.

Yet, there are ethical and philosophical barriers to consider. For example, who owns the copyright to an algorithmically generated work of art? Is it ethical to use AI to create music or art that might have an emotional impact on humans? And what if machines start 'thinking' in ways we cannot understand, developing an alien form of creativity unfathomable to the human mind?

These dilemmas force us to reevaluate our preconceptions about creativity and reconsider the role Artificial Intelligence might play in the future of creative thinking. As we continue to advance the field of Artificial Intelligence, we must proceed with caution and awareness, always keeping in mind the inestimable value of human creativity. And perhaps, just in doing so, we may discover new truths about the nature of creativity itself, whether human or artificial.

CHAPTER 2:
THE BASICS OF
CREATIVE AI.

Inside the vast world of artificial intelligence, there is one particular corner that continues to amaze and fascinate experts and laymen alike: creative AI. At first glance, creativity and algorithms might seem like two diametrically opposed concepts, like black and white on a painter's palette. But just as the painter mixes colors to create unexpected nuances, so Creative AI combines mathematical rigor and free expression to generate surprising results.

Situated at the intersection of art and science, Creative AI does not merely emulate or replicate human creativity, but offers a new way of thinking about the creative process itself. This is made possible by a subcategory of algorithms known as "generative algorithms," which are designed to produce something new from a set of input data or rules. Whether text, images, music or any other art form, generative algorithms are opening new frontiers in understanding what it means to be truly creative.

To understand the power of generative algorithms, it is essential to grasp the difference between generative models and discriminative models, the two major fields into which machine learning algorithms are divided. While discriminative models focus on labeling or classifying data-for example, identifying whether an image contains a cat or a dog-generative models go further. They seek to understand how the data were generated, thus opening the door to the creation of new data that share the same characteristics.

Imagine an artist studying the effect of light on various materials and then painting a picture that captures that light in a realistic way. Similarly, a generative algorithm "studies" input data, such as musical notes or pixels in an image, to "paint" something completely new but aesthetically consistent with the original material.

The applications are endless and transcend the boundaries of art. In industry, for example, generative algorithms are used to create optimized product designs that would otherwise have required countless hours of human labor. In medicine, they can generate molecule structures for new drugs. And, of course, in the digital art world, they are changing our concept of authorship and intellectual property.

That's the magic of Creative AI: its ability to push the limits of what we consider possible, both in terms of aesthetics and practical utility. It is not just automation or incremental improvement, but a revolution in the way we generate and think about creativity. With each algorithm perfected, with each new application discovered, a future in which humans and machines collaborate not only to solve problems, but also to explore new dimensions of imagination and inspiration, is emerging more and more clearly. Thus, Creative AI and generative algorithms are not just tools in the hands of artists or engineers; they are open windows into worlds yet to be discovered, inviting each of us to look beyond the known horizon to ask, "What else is possible?"

In a world where artificial intelligence (AI) is penetrating every field, the idea of "Creative AI" may seem, at first glance, an oxymoron. Creativity is often considered an exclusively human prerogative, a realm that machines could never hope to enter. Yet here we are at the confluence of engineering and art, where algorithms and neural networks seek to simulate, and in some cases amplify, the human creative impulse.

Exploring Creative AI requires an understanding of neural networks and deep learning, the core technologies that power this form of artificial intelligence. A neural network is a system of algorithms that attempts to recognize underlying patterns by interpreting raw data through the process of machine learning. Neural networks are structured similarly to the human brain, with interconnected nodes or "neurons" transmitting signals. A deep learning neural network, or deep neural network, is a complex variant that uses multiple layers of these neurons to interpret data.

The power of deep learning lies in its ability to learn autonomously from data, rather than following programmed instructions. This makes it ideal for generating artificial creativity. A bursting example of this is the generation of images or music. In these scenarios, the neural network "learns" from a training data set composed of examples of the type of output we wish to generate. By opening the door to variability and interpretation, the network can produce outputs that, while informed by the original dataset, are unique.

There are ethical and philosophical questions that arise when we talk about Creative AI. For example, can an algorithm really have an act of imagination? And if so, who owns the rights to that generated piece of art or music? These are questions that do not have easy answers, but they stimulate further thinking about what it means to be creative and, more generally, what it means to be human in an era dominated by artificial intelligence.

But Creative AI is not limited only to the world of art and culture. Imagine an AI system that can design new drugs or advanced materials, harnessing its "creativity" to discover combinations of molecules that scientists may not yet have considered. Or think of a virtual assistant that not only organizes your calendar, but does so in such an intuitive and personal way that it almost seems like an extension of your thinking.

To fully understand Creative AI, it is essential not only to study its practical applications, but also to immerse yourself in the ethical and philosophical debate surrounding it. As designers, engineers and artists continue to push the limits of what AI can do, it is incumbent upon us as a society to reflect on the implications of this revolutionary form of intelligence and the responsibility we have in shaping its path.

Creative AI is not merely an exercise in programming or engineering. It is a fascinating intersection of art and science, an uncharted territory where machine and human collaborate to give birth to something that is more than the sum of its parts. If traditional AI is focused on optimization and efficiency, creative AI focuses on innovation and originality.

Often the first step in delving into the world of creative artificial intelligence is selecting the right tools and software. Many might think that this is merely a technical act, almost like choosing the right brush for a painting. But the reality is that the tools and software can actually shape the kind of creativity that will be possible to express.

Take, for example, software such as TensorFlow or PyTorch. These are deep learning frameworks that offer a wide range of pre-packaged algorithms and libraries to facilitate development. But what is really exciting is that they offer incredible flexibility, allowing developers to explore new neural architectures and optimization methods that can be specifically designed for creative tasks. That's the beauty of creative AI; it is not limited by the parameters of a single application or industry.

Another key tool in creative AI is the Generative Adversarial Network (GAN). These models have the ability to "imagine" new entities based on the data they have been trained with. When fed a set of Monet paintings, for example, they can generate new works of art that capture the style and essence of the master, but are original works in their own right. This has extraordinary applications, from creating new designs for fashion to simulating environments for virtual reality.

Tools like GPT-3, on the other hand, have opened the door to textual creativity. Writers, journalists, and even songwriters are beginning to use these models to generate content that can be as emotional and compelling as that created by humans. The fascination lies in the way these machines can assimilate an enormous amount of information and produce something new, something beyond mere replication.

But not everything is tied to pure technology. The human factor remains indispensable. Tools and software are only means through which to express a vision, idea or concept. Without the expert guidance of an individual who understands both the art and science of creativity, even the most sophisticated artificial intelligence will be limited. And therein lies the real magic of creative artificial intelligence: in the synergy between the machine's ability to process data efficiently and the human intuition for beauty, emotion and meaning.

So as we explore tools and software, let us keep in mind that they are only the starting point. The real adventure begins when we accept the ongoing dialogue between human creativity and the endless possibilities offered by technology. It is a journey that promises to rewrite the rules not only of what machines can do, but also of what humanity can become.

In today's technological landscape, artificial intelligence (AI) has become a buzzword that occupies headlines, conference screens and boardroom tables. Although there are many who talk about algorithms and data, few can grasp a fundamental nuance of AI: its ability to be creative. Yes, you read that right. Algorithms can be programmed not only to perform calculations or perform logical operations, but also to generate original content, solve problems in innovative ways, and even compose music or art.

At the heart of creative AI are so-called generative algorithms, computational mechanisms designed to produce something new. For example, generative neural networks can create realistic images from scratch, while reinforcement learning algorithms can invent strategies for winning at complex games such as Go or chess, which require a high degree of strategic inventiveness. It is a fascinating world that reveals itself beyond numbers and statistics, one in which AI challenges our traditional conceptions of creativity and innovation.

This opens up a range of possibilities in terms of practical application. Take, for example, the pharmaceutical industry. Here, creative AI can help identify new molecules or drug combinations with greater efficiency and fewer side effects. Imagine an algorithm that "imagines" a novel molecule, analyzes its structure, tests it in virtual simulations and finally suggests human scientists to synthesize it for further testing. Not only does this speed up the discovery process, it also paves the way for more effective and safer treatments.

In the arts, creative AI is already an evolving reality. Algorithms can now generate works of art, compose musical pieces and even write short stories. And it is not just a simple replication or modification of the already existing; these systems are able to create something completely new, following the aesthetic or narrative principles set by their human creators. Similarly, in the world of design and architecture, generative algorithms are used to come up with unique designs, optimize the use of space, and even simulate the environmental impact of new buildings before they are built.

However, with great power also comes great responsibility. As we explore the potential of creative AI, we must also consider the ethical and social implications. Who owns the copyright to an algorithmically generated work of art? How can we ensure that artificial creativity is not used for malicious or manipulative purposes? These are questions that require deep reflection and open debate among scientists, artists, philosophers and lawmakers.

Creative AI is not just an academic concept or a technological curiosity; it is an emerging field that promises to revolutionize the way we work, create and even how we live. From developing new drugs to composing symphonies, from optimizing transportation systems to enriching our cultural experiences, the applications are as vast as they are fascinating. But to navigate this uncharted territory with wisdom and integrity, it is critical to understand not only how creative AI works, but also what its limitations, risks and incredible opportunities are. That is why education and critical reflection on this topic are more important than ever.

Artificial intelligence, or AI, is often associated with rigorously analytical and mathematical tasks, from medical diagnosis to automotive traffic management. But one of the most fascinating areas of AI development is that of creativity. Yes, we are talking about algorithms that can paint, compose music, write poetry and even come up with concepts for new designs. Let's get into the beating heart of this exciting frontier by examining the basics of creative AI and the crucial role of data and creative input.

It is critical to understand that creative AI does not arise in an isolated vacuum; it is a skillful combination of mathematical models, data representations, and learning algorithms. One of the first questions that arises is: how can a computer, a machine designed to perform computations, be "creative"? The answer lies largely in the complexity and flexibility of deep learning algorithms. These algorithms do not just learn rigid patterns; they are designed to assimilate and process information in a much more human-like way. With adequate training data, they can "learn" to make changes, innovate and even surprise.

This is where the importance of data and creative input comes in. In traditional AI, data are often numbers, statistics or other forms of quantifiable information. In creative AI, data takes on a completely different guise. We are talking about brush strokes on a canvas, musical notes in a symphony, or even the subtle emotional tones in a poem. These "creative" data provide the fertile soil in which AI can sow the seeds of creativity. Without a well-curated and highly specific data set, even the most advanced deep learning model will be barren in terms of creative capabilities.

But there is more. Once the AI model has assimilated this data, the next step is the creative interpretation and manipulation of that data. Take, for example, an AI algorithm that creates visual art. Once trained on thousands of paintings, from classical paintings to contemporary works, the algorithm can begin to generate images that incorporate elements of different styles, creating something completely new, yet remarkably familiar.

Let us not forget, however, that creative AI is not an isolated entity; it is a collaboration between man and machine. Artists, musicians, and creative people of all sorts can use AI as a tool to extend their capabilities, to explore new artistic horizons that might otherwise be inaccessible. Here's where it gets really interesting: when creative AI becomes an amplifier of human creativity, rather than a substitute for it.

The road to true creative AI is paved with ethical and philosophical challenges. Who owns the rights to an algorithmically generated work of art? What is the intrinsic value of a machine-generated musical composition? These are questions that society as a whole will face as creative AI continues to evolve and blur the lines between engineering and art, science and creativity.

Thus, as we sink into the age of creative AI, it is imperative that we look beyond the mere mechanics of algorithms and focus on the heart of the human experience: the ability to create, to innovate, and to express ourselves in ways that transcend code and computation. It is a journey that will force us to reconsider our very definitions of art, creativity and, ultimately, what it means to be human.

CHAPTER 3: AI IN MUSIC

In the contemporary artistic landscape, artificial intelligence is increasingly becoming a leading character, a kind of virtuoso that joins composers and arrangers in creating new harmonies. We are not just talking about a mere support tool, but an artistic interlocutor capable of suggesting creative cues, changing aesthetic paradigms and challenging the conventions of musical tradition.

If we detach ourselves for a moment from the preconceived notion that art is the exclusive domain of human intuition and soul, we can discover how artificial intelligence, through algorithms and machine learning, is beginning to decode the complex mathematical patterns and harmonic structures that underlie music. AI can analyze the frequency, rhythm, melody and even timbre of a composition, processing data in such detail that it becomes possible to generate new musical pieces or suggest variations on existing themes.

Consider modern DAWs (Digital Audio Workstations) that incorporate AI-based functions to aid in audio mixing or instrument selection. An arranger can use these technologies to improve the acoustics of a piece, often achieving results close to technical perfection, something that would require hours of manual labor and considerable know-how.

In the field of composition, there are algorithms that can generate musical structures from a set of rules or a database of pre-existing compositions. Some of this software can even "learn" the style of a particular composer and generate music that emulates that aesthetic. The appeal lies in the fact that as the machine learns, it can also suggest cues that might not be immediately obvious to humans, precisely because AI is free of the cultural biases and sensory limitations that characterize human perception.

However, the collaboration between artificial intelligence and human creativity raises some ethical and philosophical questions. Who owns the copyright of an AI-generated composition? Can the machine really be considered a "co-author"? And what about the sometimes-expressed fear that artificial intelligence may "replace" the human composer?

These questions are not easily answered. Perhaps the real potential of this synergy lies in creating a fruitful dialogue between human and machine, a kind of duet in which each "musician" brings his or her own unique skills. In this scenario, AI is neither a mere tool nor a substitute, but a true creative partner.

It is a fascinating era for music, a time of experimentation and discovery, in which the boundaries between technology and art are becoming increasingly permeable. Artificial intelligence is not just a tool: it is a new lens through which to explore the vast and complex universe of musical composition and arrangement, a universe in which the sum of the parts may indeed exceed all expectations.

At the intersection of art and science, artificial intelligence is revolutionizing the world of music in ways unthinkable just a few years ago. This technological development has opened doors to new forms of artistic expression, exploration and analysis, radically changing not only how music is produced, but also how it is interpreted and studied.

Think for a moment of machine learning algorithms, which today can scan an entire catalog of music and analyze it to understand its constituent elements, from vocal timbres to melodic and rhythmic structures. This kind of detailed analysis has immense implications for musicological research. For example, algorithms can uncover influences and trends among artists and genres, revealing hidden connections and thus enriching our understanding of music history. Scholars can use this information to discover and reanalyze the evolution of a style or the progression of an artist, all with unprecedented accuracy and speed.

But artificial intelligence is not limited to simple analysis. It is also changing the way music is created. AI-driven composition algorithms are opening new frontiers in musical creativity. They generate melodies, harmonies and even entire songs based on training data, which can include a wide range of sources, from classical great masters to contemporary hits. This creates a fertile environment for innovation, where musicians and composers can collaborate with AI to explore new sounds and structures. In this way, AI almost becomes an additional composer or musician, expanding creative possibilities rather than replacing the human touch.

Beyond that, AI techniques are also enhancing music recommendation and personalization. Streaming platforms such as Spotify use sophisticated algorithms to analyze listeners' preferences and suggest tracks they might like, thus creating a more engaging and personalized music experience. These algorithms can also uncover emerging talent, giving them a platform and audience they might not otherwise have.

It is critical, however, to consider the ethical and philosophical implications of this revolution. The use of technology to create or analyze art raises questions about copyright, originality, and what it really means to be an artist in the digital age. Some argue that collaboration with AI could dilute the intrinsic value of human artistic expression. But this viewpoint tends to ignore the fact that AI is simply a tool, a medium through which artists can explore new heights of creativity.

The potential synergy between artificial intelligence and music thus represents an area of research that deserves deep reflection and ongoing study. Every discovery and innovation in this space opens up new questions and possibilities. It is not only about how technology will change music, but how this unprecedented collaboration between man and machine can elevate art itself to new levels of complexity and beauty. What is certain is that the fusion of AI with music is creating an incredibly dynamic and ever-evolving landscape that will continue to influence and inspire generations of artists, researchers, and listeners.

The fusion of artificial intelligence and music is an exciting and constantly evolving arena, a marriage of science and art that has the potential to redefine both the way we understand music and our approach to machine learning. We are not simply talking about algorithms that generate personalized playlists or recommend songs based on our previous listening. The frontier is much broader, and one of the most intriguing areas is Performative AI, or artificial intelligences capable of performing dynamically and responsively.

Imagine a musical ensemble composed not only of human musicians but also of AI agents, capable of improvising in real time, adapting to the emotional flow of the performance, and collaborating with human performers as true stage companions. This is not a science fiction tale, but an emerging reality. AI tools such as these can not only interpret scores, but also 'hear' and 'respond' to human musicians, thanks to sophisticated machine learning models that analyze the timbre, rhythm and dynamics of sounds in real time.

One of the most fascinating applications of Performative AI is the possibility of expanding the boundaries of musical composition. Each artist brings with him or her a wealth of influences, styles, and techniques, but an AI agent can tap into an almost infinite database of musical information, resulting in unexpected synergies and cross-genre encroachments. AI can suggest unusual harmonic progressions, structure new types of arrangements, or even create entire pieces from simple musical fragments provided by the human.

This also has an impact in music pedagogy. The use of Performative AI as a teaching tool opens up a world of opportunities for students, who can benefit from immediate and personalized feedback. At the same time, teachers can use these tools to better understand their students' strengths and weaknesses, individualizing lessons far more effectively than traditional methods allow.

However, the convergence of AI and music is not without ethical and philosophical concerns. What place does the human artist occupy in this new ecosystem? How does the audience perceive a performance in which not all 'musicians' have physical bodies or emotions? And, even more fundamentally, can art generated by an algorithm really be considered 'art' in the traditional sense of the term?

The answers to these questions are far from simple and are fueling an increasingly heated debate among musicologists, computer scientists, and philosophers. But one thing is certain: artificial intelligence has already left an indelible mark on the world of music and will continue to do so, opening up unexplored avenues and posing questions we never thought we would have to face. The boundary between technology and art has become more permeable than ever, and the possibilities seem endless. So as we listen to the harmony produced by the symbiosis between silicones and vocal cords, it remains to be seen how this unexpected adventure will change the way we create, listen to, and experience music.

The convergence of artificial intelligence and the music world has created a soundscape that is both fascinating and full of legal and ethical unknowns. This meeting of seemingly different worlds is generating innovations ranging from composition to distribution, profoundly affecting how we perceive intellectual property and copyright.

To understand the phenomenon, it is essential to outline the horizon of AI intervention in the music industry. Algorithms, driven by powerful machine learning techniques, can now create melodies, harmonies and even lyrics. Music production, once the exclusive domain of human ingenuity, is now in a gray area, where originality is a blend of algorithmic engineering and human expression. Some platforms, such as Amper Music or AIVA, are already using AI to compose original music tracks. But what happens when an algorithm generates a melody that resembles an existing, copyrighted piece?

A first point of consideration is the question of ownership. If an algorithm creates a song, who owns the rights to that composition? Is it the programmer who wrote the algorithm? Or the user who provided the input data? Or perhaps no one, since an algorithm cannot, legally, own intellectual property? These questions take us into an unexplored land of law, where existing regulations struggle to provide satisfactory answers.

Legal uncertainty also extends to distribution. Streaming plataforms such as Spotify or Apple Music use recommendation algorithms to suggest tracks to users, thus shaping music consumption and, indirectly, artists' earnings. This raises the question of whether such algorithms should be designed to be more transparent or ethically responsible, especially when they may favor or penalize certain artists or genres.

But that is not all. AI also offers tools to monitor and manage royalties more effectively. Technologies such as audio fingerprinting can automatically identify copyrighted music and ensure that artists are properly compensated when their music is used in podcasts, videos, or other media. However, the challenge is to ensure that these technologies are used fairly and do not become tools for excessive surveillance or restriction of artistic freedom.

The rapid and unstoppable development of artificial intelligence in music presents us with a number of dilemmas that require careful consideration. It is not only a question of who owns the rights to a song, but also how those rights are exercised and protected in an increasingly digitized and globalized ecosystem. More importantly, it is a question of the very nature of art and creativity, and how these can coexist and interact with the seemingly endless possibilities offered by technology. So while we enjoy the incredible innovations that AI is bringing to the world of music, it is incumbent upon us to address these complex legal and ethical issues with the seriousness and depth they deserve.

Artificial intelligence has broken new ground in a myriad of fields, but its foray into the world of music has a special flavor, almost a harmonious anomaly. Traditionally, music has been considered the last bastion of human creativity, an art form so inherently emotional that the very idea of automating it seemed heretical. But as with many other heresies, this one has been subjected to rigorous scrutiny and, in many cases, accepted and celebrated for its distinctiveness and contributions.

Imagine for a moment an invisible composer working around the clock, generating melodies and harmonies with a click. This is not a scene from a science fiction movie, but a reality offered by applications such as AIVA, which uses deep learning algorithms to compose original music. The sophistication of these tools is such that the composition generated can be indistinguishable from that created by human hands. AIVA has even been credited as a composer in film and video game soundtracks, turning what was once exclusively human territory into a shared space of creativity.

But composition is just the tip of the iceberg. Think of big data analytics in the discovery of new talent. Platforms like Spotify use sophisticated algorithms to analyze listening patterns and predict which songs or artists will emerge as the next hits. This not only gives unknown artists a chance to get noticed, but also sharpens the user experience, who is exposed to music they are likely to love but would not have discovered otherwise.

While algorithms help us discover new music, AI tools in music production are democratizing the creative process. Software such as DADABOTS uses neural networks to create music in specific styles. With these tools, even those who are not trained musicians can produce high-quality tracks. This levels the playing field, allowing more people to express their creativity without the barrier of formal music training.

No less important is the way AI is changing the interaction with music. Virtual assistants such as Alexa or Siri can now understand and respond to complex musical requests, such as "play a sad song from the 1980s." In addition, music chatbots can assist users in finding the right music for their mood or activity, making music an even more personalized and interactive experience.

And as we explore these changes, it is critical to reflect on what it means for our concept of art and creativity. Artificial intelligence in music is not a substitute for, but a complement to, human creativity. It offers new tools and possibilities, extending the fabric of our artistic expression. As in any other field transformed by AI, the true potential will be revealed when we learn to coexist and collaborate with these tools, instead of seeing them as antagonists. And it is in this symbiosis that the bright and harmonious future of AI in music lies.

CHAPTER 4: AI IN VISUAL ART

The intersection of artificial intelligence and visual art is one of the most fertile and least explored terrains of contemporary innovation. On the one hand, we have art, an unconditional expression of human experience that has evolved through the centuries, taking such diverse forms as painting, sculpture, and drawing. On the other, artificial intelligence, a rapidly developing technological frontier that seems to be the exclusive domain of mathematicians and engineers. But what happens when these two spheres meet?

The answer is as surprising as it is fascinating. Several AI platforms are now able to generate visual works of art that are virtually indistinguishable from those created by human artists. Algorithms such as Generative Adversarial Networks (GAN) are capable of learning from a dataset consisting of existing works of art and creating new works based on this learning. Yet, the question that arises is: can these creations really be considered art? The answer is not simple and involves various factors such as intentionality, emotion and cultural perception.

Let us look at the issue of "creativity" in painting. In a human painting, every brushstroke is charged with intentionality. The artist consciously decides every aspect of the painting, from the use of color to the play of light and shadow. In the case of AI, the "decision" is left to a series of mathematical calculations. Some might argue that this takes a vital element away from the traditional definition of art, yet others see in this a new form of creativity, a kind of collaboration between man and machine that could lead to unimaginable horizons.

Let us not forget drawing, often considered the humbler relative of painting, but just as powerful in its visual and emotional impact. AI algorithms specializing in drawing already exist, and are capable of emulating styles from simple sketches to detailed portraits. Again, the question of creativity is key. While a human draughtsman can spend hours, days or even years perfecting a single work, an algorithm can generate hundreds of drawings in a fraction of a second. This raises uncomfortable questions about the value and rarity of art in an age dominated by technology.

One of the most fascinating aspects is the potential democratization of visual art through AI. The economic barriers that often prevent access to art materials can be overcome with the use of accessible AI platforms, allowing anyone with a computer to create works of art. Of course, this could have implications for the traditional art ecosystem, but it also opens a door to endless possibilities of expression for people who might otherwise not have the opportunity to explore their artistic potential.

The blending of artificial intelligence and visual art is a burgeoning field that is already changing the way we conceive of creativity, expression, and even identity. While some ethical and philosophical questions remain open, one thing is certain: the intersection of AI and art is blurring the lines between human and machine, and in this ambiguous context resides a new form of beauty, ready to be discovered and appreciated.

The soft lights of an art gallery cast soft shadows on a series of framed canvases. However, to the keen eye, something is different. Behind each work, there is an array of algorithms, a sequence of code, an artificial neural network. We are at the crossroads of art and artificial intelligence, where machines and humans meet not to compete, but to collaborate in creating something extraordinary.

In visual art, artificial intelligence is used to generate dreamscapes and detailed portraits that would be almost impossible to distinguish from works created by humans. Using detailed analysis of context and themes, these AIs are able to create works that not only fascinate aesthetically, but also challenge our understanding of art itself. They can analyze hundreds of years of art history, assimilate different styles, and then use this information to generate completely new works that are still steeped in humanity's artistic sensibility.

Turning to sculpture, artificial intelligence offers tools that can handle three-dimensionality with a previously unimaginable degree of precision. Think of the possibility of making sculptures based on detailed scans of the human form or complex mathematical models, which can be turned into reality with the help of 3D printers. Such technologies allow artists to overcome physical limitations and explore new realms of the possible.

AI does not stop at static representations; it also enters the world of interactive installations. In this context, it not only creates but "reacts," adapting in real time to the stimuli provided by visitors. These installations, powered by sensors and cameras, can change appearance, sound or even "behavior" in response to the actions of the people present. Thus, each visitor becomes a co-creator of sorts, and each interaction represents a variable that the AI incorporates in its continuous learning and adaptation process.

This is especially significant when we consider the ethical and philosophical implications of using AI in the arts. On the one hand, it could be argued that art generated by an algorithm lacks the intentionality and emotionality that only a human being can provide. On the other hand, there are those who argue that AI can actually enrich the creative process, offering new perspectives and pushing artists to explore uncharted terrain.

What is clear is that artificial intelligence is rewriting the rules of art, challenging our preconceived notions of what it means to be an artist and what art itself is. You could say that we are experiencing a kind of digital renaissance, where the barriers between science and art are becoming increasingly blurred. In this new era, artificial intelligence is not a mere tool in the hands of the artist, but rather a collaborative partner, helping to push the boundaries of human imagination to new, unexpected heights.

The dialogue between artificial intelligence and visual art represents an emerging synergy that challenges the traditional boundaries of creative expression. The interweaving of these two disciplines opens a new chapter in art history, inserting a complexity and innovative potential never seen before. Imagine a virtual canvas that is not just a simple two-dimensional space on which to lay color, but a dynamic and interactive environment that responds, learns and evolves with the artist.

Beyond the mere automation of tasks such as drawing or coloring, artificial intelligence offers a new perspective, a kind of unique dialogue with the artist. For example, "transfer style" techniques make it possible to apply the style of a famous painter to a photograph or other painting, generating results that oscillate between the purely aesthetic and the deeply evocative. This is not just a play on shapes and colors; it is a celebration of artistic complexity through the lens of mathematics and algorithms.

But this interweaving of art and technology also raises fundamental questions about the role of the artist and the nature of art itself. In a reality where an algorithm can generate visual compositions, what becomes the role of human genius? Many see this collaboration as an opportunity to extend the limits of human creativity, rather than a threat to artistic uniqueness. The artist is no longer just a creator, but also becomes a curator of ideas, an architect of algorithmic possibilities, someone who guides and directs the machine in a collaborative dance of creation.

Consider the production of digital art. Here, artworks are no longer limited by the physicality of the canvas or the chemistry of pigments. Digital art explores new mediums, such as virtual and augmented reality, providing immersive experiences that go beyond the visual to engage all the senses. A digital portrait might change expression based on the mood of its viewer, or a virtual landscape might evolve with the seasons, mimicking or even anticipating the cycles of nature.

Technology has also democratized access to art. Machine learning algorithms can help people with no artistic training to make sophisticated compositions, breaking down traditional barriers that separate "artists" from "non-artists." At the same time, artificial intelligence is giving rise to new art forms that exist only in relation to it, such as NFTs, which leverage blockchain technology to authenticate the uniqueness of a digital artwork.

Yet as we explore these new frontiers, it is crucial to reflect on how artificial intelligence can influence ethical discourse in art. The question of intellectual property is more pertinent than ever. Who owns the art generated by artificial intelligence? Is it the artist who programmed the algorithm, the machine that generated the work, or a combination of the two? And what about originality and intention, concepts so ingrained in our understanding of art?

Navigating these waters requires a holistic understanding not only of programming and design, but also of the aesthetic, ethical, and philosophical theories underlying art. In this way, the fusion of artificial intelligence and visual art is not just a technical or artistic exercise, but an interdisciplinary journey that questions the complexity of our world.

Artificial intelligence is reinventing many spheres of human life, and art is no exception to this transformation. Perhaps less obvious, but equally revolutionary, is the role of AI in the restoration and preservation of works of art. The preservation of visual art is a complex challenge involving a mix of scientific, artistic and historical expertise. Now, with the introduction of sophisticated algorithms, we can bring more effective and less invasive solutions to this process.

Imagine a situation where a historic painting, perhaps a Renaissance masterpiece, has been damaged by weather or accidents. Traditional experts would use a range of techniques to restore the work, from chemical examinations to gentle cleaning methods. However, the scope of what they can do is limited by technology and the information available to them. This is where artificial intelligence comes in.

An AI system can perform a detailed analysis of the painting, identifying the materials used, the state of preservation and even the original painting methods. This information becomes valuable tools for the restorer, who can make informed decisions about how to proceed. For example, if the algorithm identifies that a certain pigmentation was used in a damaged area, the restorer can attempt to replicate that exact color in the restoration process.

It is not just the detailed initial analysis that AI can offer. Imagine a case where a part of the painting is so damaged that it is almost unrecognizable. Here, AI can be trained to 'predict' what that area would look like if it had remained intact, based on other preserved parts of the work or even other works by the artist. This sort of 'intelligent filling' could result in a restoration more faithful to the artist's original intention.

But the scope of AI goes beyond the physical restoration of works. Preservation today also extends to the digital world. Digitizing a work of art is a complex process that requires attention to detail to accurately capture colors, textures and nuances. Artificial intelligence can enhance this process, ensuring that the digital version is as close to the original as possible. This not only facilitates access to art for a global audience, but also creates a digital archive that can be used for future restoration or research efforts.

As we explore these new horizons, it is critical to reflect on the ethics of using AI in such a sensitive context. The goal should always be to enrich the understanding and appreciation of art, rather than to replace the expert eye and skilled hand of the restorer. In this way, technology can become a complement, rather than a substitute, for the human talent and skill that have been central to the art world for so long.

Thus, artificial intelligence not only meets the practical needs of restoration and conservation, but raises intriguing questions about the intersection of technology and art. This convergence of ancient and modern, of science and aesthetics, opens an exciting dialogue that could shape the future of art and the way we perceive and preserve it for generations to come.

The art world is constantly evolving, a stage on which technology and creativity dance in an intricate duet. One of the most recent and fascinating partners in this dance is artificial intelligence. If art was once considered exclusively a human domain, today AI is opening new horizons of exploration, enriching the creative landscape in unimaginable ways.

Consider generative painting, a discipline that uses algorithms to create works of art. Artists program AI to adhere to certain aesthetic and structural rules, and the result is a collaboration in which the machine becomes a kind of co-artist. One iconic example is "Portrait of Edmond de Belamy," a portrait created by a deep learning algorithm and sold at auction at Christie's for $432,500. The news went around the world, showing how AI could also create works with economic and cultural significance.

No less fascinating is the use of AI in video art. Trained neural networks can generate intricate animations or manipulate existing videos in surprising ways. One example is the music video for Linkin Park's "In the End," recreated entirely with AI to remember the late singer Chester Bennington. In this context, artificial intelligence not only creates new art forms but also helps preserve and celebrate cultural heritage.

In addition to creation, artificial intelligence is also revolutionizing the enjoyment and preservation of art. Think of the visual recognition systems employed in museums. Algorithms can identify and catalog works of art, facilitating discovery and study. At a more advanced level, AI can also help restore damaged works of art, predicting what they would look like if they had been preserved in their original form.

What if I told you that AI could even push the boundaries of artistic interpretation? Imagine an algorithm analyzing the emotions expressed in a painting and suggesting an appropriate soundtrack. In this way, visual art and music would merge into a multisensory experience, offering audiences a deeper understanding of a work's emotional message.

But, as in any evolution, ethical and philosophical questions arise. Who owns the copyright in an AI-generated work? What is the role of the human artist in a world where machines can create? Such questions add an additional layer of complexity to the conversation, and deserve careful consideration.

In the contemporary landscape, where technology mixes with creativity in increasingly sophisticated ways, artificial intelligence in visual art represents an unexplored frontier. A frontier that raises questions, provokes debates, but above all enriches the way we see and experience art. In this dialogue between silicon and spirit, between code and brush, lies the potential for a never-before-seen artistic synthesis, a new aesthetic for a new millennium.

CHAPTER 5: AI IN LITERATURE.

Artificial intelligence, once a topic relegated to research laboratories and science fiction novels, has made its way into almost every aspect of daily life. Surprisingly, it has also found a fertile habitat in the world of literature and assisted writing. As the technology continues to grow, its impact in the literary landscape has become a fascinating intersection of humanism and science.

Imagine an aspiring writer sitting in front of his or her computer, virtual pen in hand, but inspiration seems elusive. In these situations, AI-assisted writing can function as a cybernetic muse. AI-powered writing platforms can suggest styles, tones and even plots, opening up a vortex of creative possibilities. This is not to replace the artist, but to expand his or her arsenal of creative tools. One can almost think of this as an ongoing dialogue between the creator and his digital extension, a collaboration in which each learns from the other.

One of the most fascinating aspects of this symbiosis is the role that artificial intelligence can play in improving the quality of writing itself. AI can analyze complex texts, detect inconsistencies in plot or style, and suggest changes that can turn a good story into a masterpiece. Beyond simple grammatical correction, algorithms can even provide contextual feedback on aspects such as narrative pacing, character consistency, and plausibility of events. This is an area where literary tradition and technology meet to refine the art of fiction.

Yet, it is critical to reflect on the ethical implications of such involvement. Can an algorithmically generated story be considered a work of art? And if so, who owns the rights to it? These are still open questions that require in-depth discussion by experts in the legal, ethical and artistic fields. It is essential to approach these issues with the sensitivity needed to ensure that artificial intelligence is an ally and not an adversary in the field of human creativity.

Another facet that deserves attention is accessibility. With the advent of AI-based writing platforms, even those without formal literary training can explore the world of words and ideas. This democratizes the art of writing to some extent, making it more inclusive and diverse. But it also raises the question of quality. In a world where anyone can write and publish, how do we maintain the high standards that characterize great literature?

Artificial intelligence in literature and assisted writing is a fascinating frontier that promises to reshape the contours of the human imagination. As we venture into this uncharted territory, it is crucial that we do so with a sense of curiosity but also with an unshakable ethic, balancing the infinite possibilities offered by technology with respect for the depth and complexity of the human experience. And so, as in a well-written story, the tension between man and machine offers not only conflict but also resolution, in a narrative that is yet to be written.

Artificial intelligence is revolutionizing a wide range of fields, from medicine to engineering, but one of its most fascinating and least understood applications is in the field of literature and textual analysis. Here, AI offers not only a new tool for probing texts, but also the possibility of opening horizons of understanding beyond the mere decoding of words and sentences.

When we talk about textual analysis through AI, we are referring to a complex set of algorithms and machine learning models that allow us to extract, organize and interpret information from large amounts of text. Think of Tolstoy's novels or Kant's philosophical writings; these texts can be so dense and intricate that even the most experienced of humans struggle to grasp all the nuances. AI can accelerate this process, revealing hidden patterns and semantic relationships that might escape the human eye.

An example of this potential is the automatic categorization of topics. Suppose we have a digital library of thousands of novels. An algorithm could examine these texts and categorize them according to a set of recurring themes or motifs, such as love, war, redemption, and so on. This not only facilitates search and discovery for users, but also offers scholars a new way to interrogate literature, giving them the opportunity to explore how certain themes evolve over time or vary from author to author.

Similarly, sentiment analysis, which assesses the emotions conveyed through the text, can provide valuable insights. Imagine being able to trace the emotional evolution of a character in a novel through the entire plot. Or of analyzing how emotional intensity varies in different scenes of a Shakespeare tragedy. The implications of such an approach range from literary criticism to psychology, offering new ways of understanding how literature interacts with the human mind.

But AI-driven textual analysis has broader implications as well. Think of interdisciplinary studies, where literature is often examined in relation to historical, social or political contexts. AI can help quickly identify references or concepts that are particularly salient in a given period or place, offering a more mature and multifaceted picture of the interaction between text and context.

Nonetheless, it is critical to exercise caution. Algorithms, however advanced, are not infallible and can be influenced by biases inherent in the data on which they are trained. Moreover, there is a risk of superimposing mechanical interpretations on human ones, reducing literature to a set of data to be processed, rather than as an art form that explores the human condition in all its complexities.

The synergy between artificial intelligence and literature is, therefore, a fertile field, full of promise but also of challenges. As in all human-machine relationships, success will depend on our ability to use technology to amplify our insights, rather than replace them. And so, as we continue to write and read, discuss and debate, AI will be there, a silent but powerful companion, helping us to see beyond words, into the very heart of human experience.

In contemporary literature, artificial intelligence is writing a new chapter, literally and metaphorically. One of the most intriguing and perhaps least discussed applications of this revolutionary technology is in the field of generative storytelling or, if you prefer, generative storytelling. Here, artificial intelligence does not just perform text analysis or author research; it goes further, doing the same thing humans have done around fires for thousands of years: telling stories.

Imagine an algorithm capable of constructing coherent plots, developing multidimensional characters, and setting stories in detailed realized worlds. It is true that the issue also raises a number of ethical and philosophical questions, such as the meaning of creativity and the role of the author in the storytelling process. But regardless of the dilemmas it presents, the technology of generative storytelling is offering fertile ground for exploring new narrative frontiers.

The practical applications are varied. Imagine an author struggling with so-called "writer's block." An AI algorithm could suggest various directions in which the story might evolve, freeing the author from that pesky creative impasse. Or consider the immersive worlds of video games, where stories can be driven dynamically and responsively based on player choices.

An AI could create side plots, generate realistic dialogue, and even respond intelligently to player actions, creating a gaming experience that is truly unique every time.

But it's not all sunshine and roses. As with any emerging technology, there are challenges to overcome. For example, ensuring that AI-generated language is culturally sensitive and does not perpetuate harmful stereotypes is a legitimate concern. The issue of intellectual property is another gray area: if an AI generates a story or character, to whom does that content belong? To the programmer who created the algorithm, to the user who provided the initial data, or perhaps to the AI itself?

And what about the quality of the writing? Although algorithms have become increasingly sophisticated, they often lack that emotional spark, that touch of brilliance that distinguishes a great story from a merely good one. Emotional nuance, pacing of the story, and the ability to surprise the reader are areas in which human writers excel and which, at least for now, seem to elude the ability of machines.

Despite these concerns, it is clear that artificial intelligence has much to offer the world of literature and storytelling. The possibilities are vast and largely unexplored, offering the opportunity for a true symbiosis between man and machine. In this intricate web of code and words, our understanding of storytelling, and perhaps even of ourselves, is bound to evolve in ways we can only begin to imagine today.

Artificial intelligence has infiltrated a wide range of fields, from engineering and medicine to art and literature. While the idea of a machine composing poetry or short stories once seemed like pure science fiction, today it is a tangible and constantly evolving reality. Navigating words and ideas, domains traditionally considered a bastion of human experience, has become a new horizon for advanced algorithms.

Imagine for a moment AI as a young apprentice, absorbing

styles, structures and themes from world literature. Trained on a vast digital library, this AI could generate texts in a variety of genres and styles, from epic prose to modern opera. Within this framework, the machine not only emulates the techniques of authors, but also offers new ways to experiment with form and content.

It is not just a matter of mere simulation. Artificial intelligence can generate work that pushes the boundaries of literary art. For example, some machine learning algorithms have already demonstrated the ability to create poems that capture the emotional essence of a moment, concept or experience. Algorithms can analyze linguistic and rhythmic patterns that evoke particular emotional states, enabling the creation of works that resonate with the reader at a deep level.

But there are also ethical and philosophical challenges. The question of intellectual property becomes nebulous when a machine is the author. Who owns the poetry generated by an algorithm? Is it the product of human ingenuity that trained the machine or is it a work without a defined author? Moreover, the risk of plagiarism is amplified, as the AI can generate texts that closely resemble the works it was trained on.

There is also the fear that AI may dilute the richness and complexity of human literature. If machines can write sonnets or novellas efficiently, what happens to the art of storytelling, to the uniqueness of the human voice? Let us not forget that literature is a medium through which we explore the human condition, with all its imperfections and contradictions. Can a machine, no matter how advanced, really capture that depth?

But perhaps it is in this tension between the human and the mechanical that lies the greatest potential for innovation. Artificial intelligence can act as a mirror, reflecting not only what we know, but also what we might become. It can stimulate us to question what it means to be creative, what it means to be human.

As machines learn to write, we may find that they have something to teach us as well: a new form of syntax, a new metric, or perhaps, more unexpectedly, a new form of empathy and understanding.

The intersection of AI and literature is a rapidly evolving landscape, full of possibilities and pitfalls. But one thing is certain: writing, that ancient art of expression and exploration, will never be the same again. And perhaps, in the grand scheme of things, this is something to be welcomed with curiosity rather than awe.

Artificial intelligence, a force driving innovation in fields such as medicine, engineering and industry, is also finding an increasingly relevant place in literature. It is not simply storytelling in which robots and algorithms play a role; AI is becoming an actor itself in the creative process, assisting authors and even generating content independently. This intersection of technology and creativity raises ethical and social questions worth exploring carefully.

Think, for example, of the possibility for an algorithm to write a novel. AI-assisted writing tools can suggest plots, develop characters, and even generate dialogue, freeing authors from some of the most labor-intensive stages of the creative process. But to whom do these stories belong? Does the artistic and intellectual value of a work change if an algorithm contributes significantly to its creation?

This is not just a matter of intellectual property issues; the presence of AI in the field of literature also raises broader questions related to cultural and social identity. For example, algorithms trained on large linguistic datasets may unintentionally perpetuate stereotypes and biases present in human discourse. An AI-generated novel might thus risk reinforcing problematic worldviews rather than challenging them, as great literature often aspires to do.

Consider also accessibility. If publishing houses widely adopt AI tools, it will become increasingly easy for authors to generate content at a faster pace. This could make the publishing market even more saturated than it already is, with the risk of marginalizing emerging authors who do not have access to these advanced technologies. In a world where AI becomes a common literary tool, how do we ensure that lesser-heard voices are not stifled?

Another ethical aspect concerns the emotional connection readers make with authors. Literature is a way to connect with other human minds, to explore new perspectives and engage with thoughts and feelings that may be very different from our own. If an algorithm can replicate the genius of a great writer, what happens to that connection? Will we willingly accept being moved by the words of a machine, or will we feel cheated, deprived of an authentic experience?

These questions pose challenges that go far beyond legal and commercial implications. They touch the heart of what it means to be human in an age of rapid technological change. As we continue to integrate AI into our lives, including the literary sphere, we must proceed with caution, mindful of the ethical and social impacts. Literature, after all, is a mirror reflecting the complexities of the human condition. It is vital that it continues to do so accurately and empathetically, even in the age of artificial intelligence.

CHAPTER 6: AI IN FILM AND ENTERTAINMENT

The world of film and entertainment has always been an experimental laboratory for emerging technologies. Technological evolution has never been a mere accessory, but often a catalyst for new narrative and artistic possibilities. In the contemporary context, artificial intelligence is becoming a discreet but incisive player, influencing both the creative process and the enjoyment of works.

Imagine a film production context in which an artificial intelligence algorithm is involved from the pre-production stage. It usually starts with an idea, a glimmer of a story that the author wants to bring to the screen. This is where artificial intelligence comes in, capable of analyzing thousands of scripts, identifying winning story arcs and suggesting elements that could make the story more compelling or more coherent. This is not to replace human genius, but to enrich it, providing an analytical tool that can detect patterns and trends that might elude even the most experienced screenwriter.

But the involvement of artificial intelligence does not stop at the writing stage. Think of the storyboard, that sequence of preparatory drawings used to visualize the look and feel of the film before it is made. Artificial intelligence software, specializing in interpretation and image generation, can now assist in the conception of these panels, suggesting scene compositions or even changes to the cinematography that might improve the final product.

It is not an exaggeration to say that artificial intelligence can even influence the post-production stage. Machine learning algorithms are trained to perform color grading, optimize visual effects and even help edit the film, speeding up processes that would take hours of manual work and allowing the director to focus on more creative and less technical decisions.

And what about the enjoyment of the works? In this area, too, artificial intelligence is opening up unhoped-for horizons. Streaming platforms are using sophisticated algorithms to recommend movies and TV series based on detailed analysis of users' tastes. A new genre of interactive cinema could also emerge, in which audiences, through their behavior or comments, can influence the course of the plot in real time, thanks to dynamic scripts managed by artificial intelligence.

As we explore these frontiers, it is crucial to remember that technology is a tool, not an end. Artificial intelligence in film and entertainment amplifies human capabilities, but it cannot replace the intuition, sensitivity and creative genius that are the beating heart of every great work of art. What is certain is that the boundaries between man and machine are becoming increasingly blurred, and in this intricate dialogue could be born the memorable stories of the future.

The magic behind the creation of fantastic worlds, incredible characters and breathtaking scenes in movies and entertainment is often attributed to the creative genius of artists and filmmakers. What if I told you that a significant part of this magic is generated by algorithms and artificial intelligence models? Yes, it's true; AI is revolutionizing the way we consume and produce entertainment, making digital reality almost indistinguishable from real life.

Let's start with the way AI is applied in the generation of special effects. Take, for example, motion capture technology, the technology that allows human movements to be captured and translated into digital animations. In the past, this process required heavy post-production and manual input from artists to refine every detail. Today, machine learning algorithms can analyze raw data and generate high-quality animations with minimal supervision, reducing both cost and production time.

Another spectacular advance is in the creation of digital environments. Developers are using AI to generate complex and detailed landscapes, such as intricate forests or futuristic cities, that would be too expensive or even impossible to create manually. These environments are not only visually stunning, but also dynamic; they can change in real time in response to the characters' actions, making the experience much more immersive for the viewer.

No less important is the role of AI in improving digital make-up and virtual prosthetics. For example, it is possible to realistically age or rejuvenate an actor through the use of algorithms that understand how facial features change with time. This ability to manipulate human appearance goes far beyond the boundaries of traditional prosthetics, providing filmmakers with unprecedented creative freedom.

But what really makes the use of AI in this area exciting is its ability to constantly learn and improve. Every film, every scene, every frame serves as a data set that can be used to further refine the algorithms. This means that we are only at the beginning of what can be achieved. As machine learning techniques become more sophisticated, we may reach a point where digital creations will be indistinguishable from reality.

Therefore, AI is not just a technical tool; it is a fellow traveler in the artistic quête. It represents an extension of the palette of tools available to creatives, pushing the boundaries of what is possible. While purists might argue that the intensive use of technology could diminish the human element in art, it is essential to recognize that AI is a tool, not a substitute. Artists remain at the center of the creative process; AI simply expands the possibilities available to them.

So the next time you are entranced by a scene in a movie or a stunning visual effect, remember that an algorithm may be behind that beauty, working in harmony with human genius to bring that vision to life. And it is this marriage of art and science that makes the modern age of entertainment so extraordinarily fascinating.

Imagine a world where cinematic art and the entertainment experience reach a new dimension, a level where reality and fiction seem to blend indistinguishably. This is the emerging realm where artificial intelligence (AI) meets film and entertainment. Storytelling, animation, character design, and even direction are just some of the areas where AI is leaving an indelible imprint.

If you have ever watched a modern animated film or game simulation and wondered how image rendering can be so remarkably realistic, the answer is the increasing use of AI-powered real-time rendering techniques. In its essence, real-time rendering is the instantaneous creation of images from 3D models, which become immediately visible to the user. In the past, this process required a lot of computational effort and time. Today, with the help of AI, this creation can take place in real time, making possible a new era of immersive experiences.

AI makes it possible to model virtual environments with extremely complex details. Imagine a scene in which leaves, blades of grass and even dust particles are individually rendered to replicate a visual reality. It is the dedication to detail that creates true immersion, which in turn defines the audience's experience. Convolutional neural networks and deep learning techniques are often employed to learn from texture and lighting data, enhancing realism through high-fidelity models that can be calibrated and refined in real time.

In addition to visualization, AI is also transforming the

way stories are conceived and told. AI systems can now analyze narrative structure, pacing, themes, and even emotions, suggesting ways to optimize and refine content. Some film studios are already using AI to predict a film's success before its release, based on factors such as plot, genre, and casting.

But all that glitters is not gold. The ethical issue is one component that cannot be overlooked. There is a growing debate about intellectual property when AI is involved in artistic creation. Who owns the rights to an AI-generated character or a plot suggested by an algorithm? These questions require thoughtful answers and legislative solutions.

Moreover, while AI has the potential to make entertainment more engaging and personalized, there is also the risk that the technology can be used to create deepfakes or other visual manipulations that can confuse or mislead audiences. Thus, a balance between innovation and responsibility is imperative.

And so, as we travel through this exciting landscape where artificial intelligence and film converge, we must be aware of both the enormous potential and the ethical and moral challenges that emerge. It is a delicate balance that requires the participation of artists, technologists, legislators and, most importantly, the public itself. AI in film and entertainment is not just a matter of technological improvement, but represents a new frontier of human creativity, one that invites us all to be both spectators and participants in shaping the future of art and culture.

Artificial intelligence is a silent but increasingly pervasive force that is changing the face of many industries. Among them, film and entertainment are experiencing a Copernican revolution thanks to AI. The contribution of this technology goes far beyond the automation of routine tasks; it creeps into the subtlest folds of film and entertainment content creation, distribution and marketing.

Imagine the complexity of making a film. In addition to

storytelling and art, there is a huge subtext of data analysis. At an early stage, artificial intelligence can analyze scripts and plots, comparing them with previous successful films to suggest changes that might increase commercial appeal. At the same time, deep learning algorithms are employed to refine post-production, from color correction to creating increasingly convincing special effects.

And while editing rooms are inhabited by AIs collaborating with humans, in the outside world, other algorithms are working to understand audiences. Streaming platforms, for example, are using AI to analyze user behavior: what they watch, when they stop watching, what scenes prompt them to share content. This data becomes critical in distribution planning. Why send a movie to a theater if the algorithm predicts it will be more successful online?

When we talk about marketing, artificial intelligence has become a game changer. Algorithms can analyze huge data sets to identify emerging trends, allowing producers and distributors to tailor promotional campaigns to target audiences. At a more advanced level, AI technology can generate customized movie trailers based on demographics and individual tastes. It is not just about showing the right advertisement to the right person, but showing the right version of the advertisement to the right person.

But as we become fascinated by these extraordinary developments, it is good to ponder some ethical and philosophical questions. To what extent is it ethical to use algorithms to shape content according to audience tastes? Do we risk creating a vicious cycle of conformity, where uniqueness and creative diversity are sacrificed on the altar of algorithmic efficiency? And what does it mean for the future of creative work if much of the production, distribution and marketing process can be automated?

These questions require deep reflection. As artificial intelligence continues to permeate the film and entertainment industry, it is essential to maintain an open dialogue about how this technology should be deployed. It is not just about maximizing profit or efficiency, but about understanding how AI can serve as a tool to enrich our cultural experience without draining it of its inherent human value.

In the current context, artificial intelligence is not just a technological accessory but a silent player that is redefining the rules of the game. As in any compelling story, its role could be that of hero or villain, depending on how we choose to use it. And this is a script that we all, as a society, have a duty and responsibility to write carefully.

The world of film and entertainment is undergoing a radical transformation thanks to artificial intelligence (AI). Once relegated to video editing and color correction tasks, AI now manifests itself in ways that are as subtle as they are revolutionary, penetrating both the creation and distribution of content.

Consider script writing. AI algorithms can analyze hundreds of thousands of films to identify patterns of success. Elements such as pacing, structure and even dialogue can be optimized. This is not to replace the human touch, but to amplify it. One of the best known examples is the case of Benjamin, an AI who wrote a short screenplay entitled "Sunspring," with results that, although somewhat surreal, were intriguing and full of potential.

Let's move on to the production phase, where the AI is engaged in creating special effects. For example, deep learning algorithms are able to generate photorealistic virtual environments with an accuracy and speed that exceeds human accuracy and speed. This not only reduces costs but also enables the exploration of new storytelling frontiers. The film "Gemini Man" with Will Smith used AI to create a younger version of the actor, delivering a convincing performance that would have been nearly impossible with makeup alone or traditional CGI.

No less fascinating is the use of AI in post-production. Algorithms can reduce background noise, optimize sound, and even perform initial editing, freeing creative professionals from repetitive tasks to focus on more artistic and meaningful decisions.

AI also impacts the way content is distributed and consumed. Streaming platforms such as Netflix and Spotify use sophisticated recommendation algorithms to personalize the user experience. It is no coincidence that, according to some estimates, 80 percent of views on Netflix come from algorithm-generated recommendations. Such algorithms use a multitude of data, from viewing duration to favorite genres, to predict with frightening accuracy what we would like to watch or listen to next.

One interesting case study is from Disney, which used AI to analyze viewers' facial expressions during test screenings. The data collected helped refine editing, pacing and even specific scenes to maximize emotional impact.

But AI is not without its ethical dilemmas, especially in the field of entertainment. For example, what will be the fate of professionals if machines can perform the same tasks in less time and at no cost? And what about the implications of extreme personalization of content, which could reinforce echo chambers and cultural divides?

These questions raise a serious question about the role of AI in shaping our cultural and creative future. Nonetheless, the evolution of AI in film and entertainment represents a compelling chapter in the continuing interplay between technology and art, a symbiosis that, if navigated carefully and consciously, has the potential to enrich our collective experience of the world in yet unimaginable ways.

CHAPTER 7: AI IN FASHION

The world of fashion is an ever-evolving universe, fueled by the flair of designers, the fervor of stylists, and technological innovation. And when we talk about technological innovation, we cannot ignore the increasingly pervasive role of artificial intelligence (AI) in this field. While the heart of fashion once pulsated solely in the hands of skilled tailors and visionary designers, today AI has entered the scene as a co-player influencing at multiple levels, from design to retail.

In the fashion ecosystem, AI-assisted design represents one of the most fascinating yet least understood applications. It is easy to think of AI as a kind of substitute for human talent, a machine that generates sketches or three-dimensional models. But in reality, the real power of AI lies in its being an extender of human capabilities, an amplifier of creativity.

Imagine a designer faced with the dilemma of creating a collection for the next season. In a world without AI, he would have to do market research, study trends, materials, colors and, above all, trust his instincts. With AI, however, these processes can be automated and refined. Predictive analytics tools can peer into billions of pieces of data from social media, online sales platforms, and trade magazines, and provide accurate insights into emerging trends. But that's not all. AI can also suggest combinations of materials and fabrics that might be more sustainable or cost-effective, without compromising the aesthetics or quality of the final product.

One of the most exciting aspects is customization. AI can help designers create garments that are not only aesthetically pleasing but also customized to the customer's specific needs or preferences. Through the analysis of data and behavioral patterns, AI can suggest design patterns that might have a particular impact on the target group. This level of personalization was unthinkable just a few years ago and represents a revolution for both manufacturers and consumers.

Another area where AI is helping is sustainability. Using advanced algorithms, it is possible to optimize the use of materials, reducing waste and increasing efficiency in terms of production. In addition, AI can help with supply chain traceability, ensuring that materials are from sustainable sources.

Now, it is natural to ask some ethical questions: what will happen to the role of humans in all this? Is there a risk of a loss of authenticity, of the human touch that made fashion an art? It is a debate that deserves attention. However, it is crucial to understand that AI is not here to replace human genius, but to enhance it. In a world where the demands for customization, sustainability and innovation are increasingly pressing, artificial intelligence presents itself as a tool that can help the fashion industry respond to these challenges in a more effective and inspired way.

The intersection of AI and fashion is therefore fertile territory, rich in possibilities and open questions. To successfully navigate this new landscape, a holistic approach that integrates technological expertise and creative sensibilities, with a strong awareness of ethical and social implications, is essential. Thus, AI in fashion is not only an example of how technology is changing the rules of the game, but also a model for how these rules can be rewritten in ways that are more equitable, sustainable, and ultimately humane.

Imagine a world where the catwalks of Milan, Paris or New

York are a data lab, a theater where every dress, every fabric and every color has been optimized by artificial intelligence. We are not talking about a distant future, but a rapidly evolving current landscape. The entry of artificial intelligence into the fashion industry represents a breakthrough as subtle as it is revolutionary, capable of redefining the dynamics of an entire industry.

A first aspect to consider is design. For years, designers have played with textures, colors, and shapes to create clothes that embody an idea, a feeling, or a worldview. Today, advanced algorithms can analyze images, historical data, and even social media reactions to suggest combinations of elements that might be eye-catching or innovative. Machines can process an unimaginable amount of data for a human being, offering a kind of creative collaboration between artist and technology.

It is not only design that benefits from this evolution. The life cycle of a garment, from conception to production to sale, is steeped in opportunities for the application of artificial intelligence. Automated systems for detecting defects in fabrics, for example, are improving production quality, while inventory optimization algorithms are helping retailers reduce waste by keeping the right sizes and colors in stock.

And then there is the increasingly demanding and informed consumer, who is looking for a tailored shopping experience. Here, machine learning techniques come into play to personalize the customer experience. From product recommendations based on previous purchases or browsing behaviors, to the virtualization of changing rooms where customers can "try on" clothes in a digital environment, the possibilities are immense and ever-evolving.

But what does this all mean for the future of fashion? One likely scenario is an increasing democratization of design, where creations are no longer the exclusive product of an elite of designers, but the result of a collaboration between human creativity and algorithmic analysis. Trends could emerge and fade with unprecedented speed, fueled by a continuous feedback loop between consumers and algorithms.

This new paradigm is not without challenges. There is a risk that the reliance on data and algorithms could somehow "detract" from the art inherent in fashion creation, making it a purely numerical matter. In addition, large-scale data collection and analysis raise ethical issues related to privacy and security.

However, to ignore the rise of artificial intelligence in the fashion world would be imprudent. AI is here to stay, and its impact will be felt throughout the value chain-from designers' sketches to stores to everyone's wardrobes. What is certain is that we are only at the beginning of this adventure, and the possibilities are as endless as the wardrobe AI is beginning to imagine for us. As with any innovation, the key will be finding a balance: a meeting point between the art of fashion and the science of data. Thus, as we flip through the pages of fashion magazines or walk through stores, we are not just looking at clothes; we are witnessing a silent but profoundly meaningful revolution.

Imagine a world in which the clothes you wear are designed, sewn and distributed by a system driven by artificial intelligence (AI). Does that sound like a science fiction movie concept? Yet this is a reality that is increasingly coming to fruition, thanks to the transformative power of AI applied to fashion, manufacturing, and logistics.

Artificial intelligence is not just a glamorous accessory in the fashion world; it is a driving force that is revolutionizing the industry in ways we could not have imagined even a decade ago. Take, for example, the design phase of clothing. AI platforms can analyze huge amounts of data on fashion trends, consumer desires, and even weather patterns. Using this data, algorithms can suggest designs and styles that are not only fashionable, but also adaptable to the specific needs of different demographics and seasons.

But the real magic begins when we move from design to production. Here, AI has the power to make processes more efficient and sustainable. Algorithms can calculate the exact amount of material needed for each garment, thus reducing waste. AI-driven robots can make precise cuts and seams, increasing quality and reducing production time. This not only achieves time and resource savings, but also paves the way for more ethical and sustainable fashion.

The challenge does not stop there. Once the clothes are produced, they must reach the stores and, ultimately, the consumers. This is where logistics comes in, another area where AI is making great strides. Intelligent systems can accurately predict demand at different stores, optimizing resource allocation. AI can also manage inventory in real time, identify inefficiencies in the supply chain and suggest solutions.

Think of the benefits this has not only for producers, but also for consumers. The ability to predict demand means that you are less likely to be faced with empty shelves when looking for that particular piece you had in mind. At the same time, greater efficiency in production and distribution translates into reduced costs, benefits that can be passed on to the consumer in the form of more affordable prices.

This interconnected, AI-optimized world in fashion, manufacturing and logistics is a rapidly evolving universe that requires deep and ongoing understanding. It is an invitation to look beyond the fashion horizon and see the endless possibilities that emerge when aesthetics, technology and intelligence are combined. It's not just about better-looking clothing or better-organized warehouses. It's about how AI is changing the way we think, act and interact in one of the world's most dynamic and influential industries.

At every step, from fabric fibers to barcodes on packages, AI is there, silent but powerful, ready to guide us toward a smarter, more sustainable and personalized future. And as the fashion industry continues to evolve, one thing is certain: artificial intelligence is not just a passing trend, but a profound transformation that will shape the industry for years to come.

In the current landscape of innovation and technological advancement, artificial intelligence (AI) is slowly permeating a variety of industries, profoundly changing the way they operate. One of the most fascinating, but perhaps least obvious, domains in which AI is having an impact is the fashion industry. And when it comes to fashion, one element that is gaining increasing relevance is sustainability. Combine these two seemingly divergent concepts, and a new frontier of opportunities and challenges opens up.

Imagine for a moment the journey of a garment, from conception to production. Initially, designers and creatives confront each other to bring to life a design that captures attention and reflects current or future trends. Here, AI algorithms can analyze large volumes of data to predict what the next trends will be, enabling fashion houses to produce clothes that are not only aesthetically pleasing, but also in tune with market demand. This more focused process can reduce the number of garments produced in vain, contributing to less waste production.

But sustainability is not just about waste reduction. With the help of AI, resource utilization in the production process can be optimized. For example, sophisticated algorithms can calculate the most efficient way to cut fabric to minimize waste. The supply chain can also be made more sustainable through the use of AI. Sensors and monitoring algorithms can track the environmental impact of every stage of production, from fiber cultivation to final distribution, enabling companies to make informed decisions to reduce their carbon footprint.

But let's go beyond production and consider the consumer experience. With the advancement of AI technologies such as virtual and augmented reality, customers can virtually try on clothes before they buy them. This not only improves the customer experience, but also reduces the number of returns and, consequently, the amount of items that end up in landfills.

One of the less explored, but highly promising, aspects is the use of AI in post-consumer. Imagine an app that uses machine learning to suggest to clothing owners various ways to reuse or recycle their old clothes, or how to pair them in innovative ways to create new outfits. Not only would this reduce the volume of clothes that are thrown away, but it could also awaken a new awareness about the lasting value of each piece of clothing.

The intersection of artificial intelligence and sustainability in fashion is a still partly unexplored avenue, full of potential and implications not only economic but ethical and environmental. It offers the possibility of restructuring a notoriously wasteful industry into a more efficient and planet-friendly one. AI is not a panacea, but an influential player that, if used conscientiously and responsibly, can play a significant role in shaping a more sustainable fashion future. And as consumers, it is incumbent upon us not only to embrace these innovations, but to actively demand fashion that is beautiful, sustainable and intelligent.

Artificial intelligence has permeated countless areas of daily and professional life, becoming a key player in redefining the way we live, work and interact with the world around us. One of the areas where this revolution is less obvious, but no less significant, is the world of fashion. From a superficial point of view, the combination of technology and fashion might seem forced, but the intersection of these two worlds is actually loaded with profound social and cultural implications.

Think, for example, of global supply chains. Artificial intelligence can optimize the production, distribution, and sale of garments so effectively that it cuts costs and makes "fast" fashion accessible to ever larger segments of the population. But it also leads to ethical issues regarding environmental sustainability and working conditions in developing countries. It is an ambivalent power: on the one hand, it democratizes access to goods previously considered luxury, and on the other hand, it enhances an often unsustainable and unequal system of production.

Shifting the focus from the macro to the micro, AI is also critical in the evolution of the consumer experience. Algorithms can now predict fashion trends with impressive accuracy, personalizing purchase recommendations to reflect not only individual preferences but also emerging cultural movements. While this extreme personalization is seen as a plus for the customer experience, it also risks creating cultural echo chambers in which individuals are exposed only to what an algorithm deems to be their tastes or ideological affinities.

More intriguing is the use of AI in designing clothes and accessories. Designers are beginning to collaborate with algorithms to create pieces that go beyond simple aesthetics, incorporating features that respond to external stimuli such as changing temperature or humidity. In this way, fashion is no longer just a style statement or a sign of social belonging, but an almost biological extension of ourselves, adapting and responding to our environment in real time.

And then there is the impact on cultural identity. In an increasingly globalized world, fashion is one of the last bastions of local cultural expression. But what happens when algorithms, trained on data that often reflect a Western or Eurocentric worldview, come into play? There is a risk of a kind of "algorithmic homologation," in which cultural specificities are flattened in favor of more universally accepted trends.

These are just some of the aspects in which artificial intelligence is redefining the field of fashion, with effects that go far beyond textiles and penetrate deeply into the social and cultural fabric of our world. It is a fascinating frontier, but also one loaded with ethical and philosophical questions that we are still just beginning to formulate. What is certain is that the fusion of artificial intelligence and fashion is now irreversible, and its implications, however ambivalent, will be a key topic of discussion for years to come.

CHAPTER 8: AI IN USER EXPERIENCE DESIGN.

In the modern era of digitization, artificial intelligence (AI) is becoming a driving force in numerous fields, from medicine to finance. But one of the areas where AI is showing considerable impact is user experience (UX) design. Yes, the sophisticated technology that was once seen only as the domain of engineers and data scientists is now transforming the way we interact with digital platforms, making each experience more fluid, intuitive and personalized.

The first question that arises is: how can AI really improve UX design? It seems that AI and UX belong to two completely different worlds: the former is rooted in complex algorithms and calculations, while the latter focuses on human psychology and interaction. The answer lies in integration. AI can analyze huge amounts of data faster and more effectively than any human, identifying patterns and trends that may not be immediately apparent. This data can then be used to inform design decisions, making the interface more efficient and enjoyable to use.

Take personalization as an example, a concept we are all now familiar with thanks to the relentless advancement of technologies. AI can track user behavior, from the pages they visit to the products they view, to generate highly specific recommendations. This not only increases the chances of user engagement, but also creates an experience unique to each individual. Imagine entering an online store that shows you only the products you might be interested in, eliminating the need to scroll through hundreds of irrelevant options. This is data-driven, AI-powered UX design.

But personalization is not the only aspect where AI and UX converge. Consider chatbots, now a common element in websites and applications. They are not just a way to automate customer service; they are also a tool for improving UX. A well-designed chatbot can guide users through a website, provide immediate answers to their questions and even anticipate their needs, all contributing to a smoother and more enjoyable user experience.

There is an ethical aspect to consider when it comes to AI in user experience design. Personalization, if taken to the extreme, could theoretically lead to the creation of "filter bubbles," in which users are exposed only to content and information that reinforces their preexisting beliefs. This is a challenge that UX designers and AI developers must address carefully and responsibly.

So as AI makes its way into the field of user experience design, it is essential to remember that its function is not to replace human touch, but to amplify it. The ultimate goal remains the same: to create experiences that not only satisfy, but enchant users. With the right balance of data analysis and human intuition, AI offers a wide range of tools that can make it a reality.

Human-computer interaction has long been a subject of fascination and study. In the early days of the computer age, user experience (UX) design focused primarily on efficiency and functionality. With the advent of artificial intelligence (AI), however, the landscape has changed dramatically, opening up a world of innovative possibilities and challenging established norms.

Take personalization, for example. No longer is it just a friendly face or an initial greeting on your screen. AI can now analyze user-generated data in real time to deliver an absolutely tailored experience. Imagine an online shopping application that not only recognizes your style preferences, but also anticipates your future needs based on weather patterns, upcoming events in your area, or even fluctuations in the economy. We are talking about a system so advanced that it can almost read the user's mind.

In addition to personalization, AI has had a significant impact on usability and accessibility. Speech recognition technologies, such as virtual assistants, have made interaction with technology more fluid and intuitive, particularly for users who may have difficulty with traditional inputs such as keyboards and touchscreens. These assistants can learn from the context, the user's speech patterns, and even vocal tones to provide a more human and accurate response.

But let's not stop there. Consider the ethical implications of this increasingly close symbiosis between human and machine. The algorithms that drive these tailored experiences could, without proper control, reinforce existing biases or invade user privacy. This is a crucial consideration for UX designers using AI: how do we balance innovation with ethical responsibility? AI privacy and ethics guidelines must be integrated from the earliest stages of product design, and cannot be retrospective thinking.

AI's unique ability to process and analyze large amounts of data also offers opportunities to test and improve user experience design more effectively and quickly than in the past. Machine learning systems can perform large-scale A/B testing, analyze results, and implement changes in near real-time, offering speed and efficiency that were unthinkable just a few years ago.

All this is just the tip of the iceberg. As AI continues to evolve, user experience design will be expected to become increasingly sophisticated, intuitive, and personalized. This presents a challenge for designers, certainly, but it is also an extraordinary opportunity. We are at the beginning of a new era in which technology is not just a tool we use, but an active partner in shaping our daily experiences. And like any good relationship, it will require empathy, understanding and, above all, the ability to listen and adapt. Experts and UX design professionals with a deep understanding of artificial intelligence will be the ones to lead this new wave of responsible and engaging innovation.

Diving into the world of user experience design (UX Design) is like entering a maze of human needs, wants and expectations. At every turn, there are crucial details to consider, from ease of navigation to intuitive interaction and aesthetic gratification. But what happens when this intricate web of factors merges with artificial intelligence? An almost infinite horizon of possibilities opens up, and with it come new ethical and practical challenges.

Before diving into the symbiosis of AI and UX Design, it is vital to understand the essence of both fields. Artificial Intelligence is not just a set of algorithms; it is an attempt to replicate human intuition through computation. On the other hand, user experience design is not just about how beautiful or functional a product looks, but rather about embodying an idea in an interface that meets the user's needs.

Now, imagine condensing the immense power of AI into the delicate balance of user experience design. Yes, we're talking about increasingly intelligent chatbots that can interpret users' emotional tone, recommendation algorithms that dynamically learn users' preferences to make increasingly accurate suggestions, and predictive interfaces that anticipate users' needs before they even express them.

But the real fascination lies in the subtle interactions that AI can shape, influencing not only user behavior but also user perception. Take, for example, a fitness application that uses AI to analyze the user's biometric data. In addition to providing exercise suggestions, the app could adapt the entire layout and interactions based on the user's stress or energy level, creating a unique and personalized experience.

But with great power, as they say, also comes great responsibility. The implementation of AI in user experience design raises ethical and practical issues ranging from privacy to inclusiveness. AI is capable of collecting and interpreting sensitive data, so it is imperative to address data protection concerns. In addition, the exclusive use of algorithms could generate bias and discrimination, challenging the fundamental goal of inclusive design.

The road ahead is still long and filled with uncertainties, but one thing is certain: the combination of AI and user experience design has the power to redefine the way we interact with technology and, ultimately, with the world around us. It is not just about making things easier, faster or more beautiful, but about creating experiences that are truly meaningful and reflect the complexity and diversity of the human experience.

So as designers and engineers face these challenges, it is critical that users are also aware of and participate in this journey, because in the end, every interface, every pixel, every line of code is a small step toward a future where technology is not just a tool, but an integral part of our humanity.

Artificial intelligence and user experience design are two worlds that may seem at polar opposites, and yet, the intersection between the two is a crucible of endless possibilities. Especially when we talk about accessibility, the contribution of artificial intelligence goes beyond mere automation and touches deeper spheres such as empathy, equity, and inclusion.

User experience (UX) is no longer just about the aesthetics or navigability of a website. In an increasingly interconnected world, UX becomes the key to making technologies accessible to everyone, regardless of each person's ability or disability. When we talk about accessibility in design, we are talking about design that transcends physical and cognitive limitations, giving all users equal and independent access to information and functionality.

And this is precisely where artificial intelligence comes into play. Take voice recognition systems, such as virtual assistants, for example. These technologies, based on machine learning algorithms, have become indispensable tools for people with developmental disabilities. We are talking about individuals who may have difficulty using a keyboard or mouse, but can still surf the web or control smart devices through simple voice commands.

But the application of AI in user experience design goes far beyond voice recognition. Consider chatbots, often powered by natural language processing (NLP) algorithms. Not only do they offer immediate support, but they can be programmed to recognize signs of frustration or confusion in the user's language, adapting their responses accordingly. This linguistic sensitivity can make the difference between an average user experience and a truly engaging and personalized experience.

Let's not forget advances in computer vision, which open new doors to accessibility. Applications that use computer vision to interpret and describe images and videos are becoming empowering tools for users with visual impairments. And if you think these are just futuristic applications, you are wrong. Today, thanks to AI, it is possible for a blind person to "read" a book or "see" a painting in a museum through automatically generated audio descriptions.

It is crucial, however, to address a critical reflection on the ethical role of AI in accessibility. Algorithms learn from data, and if these data reflect biases or inequalities present in society, there is a risk that AI will perpetuate these injustices rather than mitigate them. Therefore, as we explore the enormous potential of AI in UX and accessibility, we must also maintain a holistic view that considers the social and cultural impact of these technologies.

The marriage of artificial intelligence and user experience design has the potential to change the way we interact with the digital world. But as in any good marriage, it takes understanding, adaptability, and constant dialogue to ensure that both sides help build a more inclusive and accessible future for all.

In the design universe, artificial intelligence has become a silent but impactful force that is reshaping the boundaries of user experience. At first glance, design and artificial intelligence may seem distant, almost irreconcilable disciplines. Design is seen as an art, steeped in empathy and deep understanding of human behavior, while artificial intelligence is frequently associated with rigid algorithms and data analysis. Yet when these two spheres converge, a kind of alchemy occurs that can radically transform our interaction with digital platforms.

Take, for example, a fitness app. Traditionally, the user experience in that context is based on a set of predefined elements: activity tracking, workout plans, real-time feedback, and so on. But imagine an app that goes further, using AI to personalize every aspect of the experience. Here, AI analyzes historical data, observes user habits, and anticipates user needs, offering proactive suggestions and tailored workout plans. This is no longer a standard product; it is a personal digital coach that understands, learns, and adapts to the user.

In an illuminating case study, design firm IDEO partnered with a hospital to use AI in improving the patient experience. Rather than simply digitizing existing processes, they used machine learning algorithms to analyze vast datasets on interactions between patients and healthcare staff. This information was then used to train a chatbot to efficiently answer patients' frequently asked questions, freeing up valuable staff time while providing accurate and timely information to patients. The result? A significant increase in patient satisfaction and more effective use of hospital resources.

Another area where AI is revolutionizing user experience design is in the fashion industry. AI systems using computer vision techniques are transforming the way users search for and purchase clothing online. Instead of scrolling through endless lists of products, users can now upload a photo of the desired outfit and AI will find similar items from different stores, facilitating a more engaging and personalized shopping experience.

These examples illustrate how AI can be used to create more intuitive, efficient and rewarding user experiences. But the real magic happens when designers become aware of the capabilities and limitations of AI, using it not as a substitute for human ingenuity but as a powerful extender of it.

The key, then, is a synergistic collaboration between design and artificial intelligence. In this marriage of discipline and technology, design provides the vision and empathy, while AI provides the tools to realize these visions in a scalable and efficient way. The result is a user experience that is both human and remarkably advanced, one that places the individual at the center of an ever-evolving digital ecosystem. This is the future of user experience design, a future in which AI is not merely a performer, but a collaborative partner in creating better, more welcoming worlds.

CHAPTER 9: THE ETHICAL CHALLENGES OF CREATIVE AI.

In the enchanting and complex world of artificial intelligence, the creative dimension is becoming increasingly prominent. Think of artwork generated by algorithms, music composed by software, and lyrics written by increasingly sophisticated machines. These innovations represent a new frontier, not only technological, but also ethical and legal. Creative AI challenges our traditional concept of authorship, opening up debates about copyright and attribution that were previously unthinkable.

One of the most pressing issues is intellectual property. Who owns the rights to an algorithmically generated work? Is it the engineer who programmed the AI, the user who activated the algorithm, or could it even be the AI itself, although this is a controversial and widely debated perspective? Copyright law, in many countries, was conceived at a time when AI had not yet shown its creative potential; therefore, adapting existing legal principles to this new context is a challenge that has profound implications.

Ethical considerations are intertwined with these legal issues. Attribution, for example, becomes a slippery slope. If an algorithm "learns" to write poetry by analyzing the works of a famous poet, is it ethical to attribute creation solely to the algorithm? Or should one somehow acknowledge the contribution of the original poet, whose work 'nurtured' the AI? Such questions become even more complex when we think of forms of AI that can process input from multiple sources, making attribution not only difficult, but sometimes almost impossible to determine.

The concept of "accountability" also gains new nuances. When a creative algorithm produces something controversial or even offensive, who is to be held accountable? The programmers of the algorithm may not have foreseen such an outcome, and the end user may be completely unaware of the technical details that led to the creation of the work in question. Blame is thus diluted in a chain of interactions so intricate that responsibility is difficult to pin down.

Another important aspect is the democratization of art and creativity. On the one hand, AI opens up new opportunities for anyone with access to these technologies. On another, it poses the risk of an impoverishment of human creativity if too much emphasis begins to be placed on algorithmic production. Creativity is a hallmark of the human experience, and it is critical to carefully weigh how machines enter this space.

If the challenges are enormous, the possibilities are equally exhilarating. Creative AI could expand our artistic and intellectual horizons, allowing us to explore new ways of expression and better understand human nature and creativity itself. But to successfully navigate these uncharted waters, it is essential that law and ethics evolve hand in hand with technology. Only then can we ensure that the advent of creative AI enriches, rather than impoverishes, our cultural and artistic heritage.

Creative AI is an emerging subdiscipline that raises fundamental questions about the nature of ingenuity, art, and, ultimately, human beings themselves. From algorithms that compose symphonies to systems that generate visual works of art, creative AI is changing the landscape of innovation in profound ways.

But as with any revolutionary technology, ethical challenges are inevitable and require serious consideration.

Bias is one of the most pressing issues facing AI. At a fundamental level, bias in an algorithm is often the result of unbalanced training data. If an algorithm is trained on a dataset that contains biases, the system will learn those biases and perpetuate them. For example, if a creative writing algorithm is trained only on Western literature, the result will be an AI with a narrow view of global culture. Eliminating bias is not only an ethical imperative but also a prerequisite for genuine innovation in creative AI.

Parallel to bias, discrimination is another issue that requires examination. While bias can be unintentional, discrimination occurs when these biases inform decisions that negatively impact specific individuals or groups. Think of an AI algorithm used in human resources to analyze job applications: if the algorithm has been trained on a dataset that favors a certain gender or ethnicity, this can lead to discriminatory hiring decisions. The ethical implications are enormous and can have long-term repercussions not only for the individuals discriminated against but also for society as a whole, which loses the input of brilliant minds simply because of algorithmic biases.

In the context of creativity, AI also presents challenges related to authority and intellectual property. Who owns the rights to an algorithmically generated work of art? Is it the engineer who designed the algorithm, the data provider, or perhaps the user who provided the initial command? These questions challenge existing intellectual property regulations and call for new legal and ethical models.

In addition to these considerations, there is the issue of transparency. Many of the most advanced techniques in AI, such as deep neural networks, are notoriously difficult to interpret, making it nearly impossible to understand how the algorithm arrived at a particular decision or creation. In a world where human understanding is central to accountability, lack of transparency is a significant ethical hurdle.

These dilemmas are not unsolvable, but require a multidisciplinary approach involving ethicists, engineers, artists, and lawyers. Public discussion is equally crucial. As a society, we must decide what values we want our technology to reflect, because creative AI, like any other form of creativity, is ultimately a mirror of our collective aspirations, prejudices, and values.

When we talk about creative artificial intelligence (AI), it is easy to think of the exciting applications that are revolutionizing fields such as art, design, and music. But as we celebrate this incredible technological evolution, it is crucial not to forget the looming ethical issues and the inevitable impact on employment.

Creative AI challenges the traditional boundaries of intellectual property. An algorithm can generate a piece of music or a work of art, but who really owns that work? In a world where creative contributions can be both human and machine, the line between originality and imitation becomes increasingly blurred. At the same time, we also face questions about the moral authorship of these creations. If an algorithm creates a work of art that is culturally insensitive or controversial, who is responsible? Having an AI system that can create at human levels raises ethical questions not only about responsibility, but also about the importance of preserving the integrity and uniqueness of human ingenuity.

These questions are intricately intertwined with the problem of employment. As creative AI improves, there will be an increasing overlap with jobs previously considered an exclusively human domain. Graphic designers, copywriters, and even compositors are already beginning to feel the brunt of algorithmic competition. The danger here is twofold: diminishing job opportunities for creative professionals and a possible erosion of quality in the creative production field. Algorithms, while advanced, cannot (at least for now) emulate the deep emotional and cultural context that a human being brings to a creative project. There may be a risk that, in attempting to automate the creative process, we may lose elements of human sensitivity and complexity.

Nor can we ignore the implications of social class and accessibility. Creative AI technologies, in general, are proprietary and expensive. This could lead to a kind of creative elitism, in which only those who can afford these advanced resources will have a chance to compete in the marketplace. This could further exacerbate existing inequalities in the world of work and beyond.

But not everything is doom and gloom. We should also consider the potential for closer collaboration between humans and machines. With the right governance, creative algorithms could act as tools that extend our capabilities, rather than as substitutes. In that case, ethics would require that these technologies be designed and implemented in ways that enhance human ingenuity rather than replace it, while ensuring equitable and democratized access.

As we continue to navigate the still uncharted sea of creative AI, it is imperative that ethics and humanism be our helmsmen. The decisions we make today will shape not only the future of the creative sector but will profoundly affect the moral texture of our society. So as we embrace the incredible opportunities presented by these advanced technologies, we must act with the utmost awareness of the ethical responsibilities they entail.

As artificial intelligence continues to advance, becoming increasingly sophisticated and capable of emulating human behavior, new ethical and legal challenges emerge that can no longer be ignored. One of the most intriguing areas is that of creative AI: software that can compose music, write poetry and even paint pictures. But what happens when a machine creates something that is traditionally attributed to human ingenuity?

Who owns the rights to these creations, and how do we handle the ethical implications that arise from these questions?

When we talk about creative AI, copyright is often the first legal issue that comes to mind. Normally, the creation of a work of art or piece of music is protected by copyright, granting the creator exclusive rights over distribution and monetization. However, in the context of AI, determining intellectual property becomes a slippery slope. If software composes a symphony or writes a novel, who is the real author? Is it the engineer who programmed the algorithm, the user who provided the input data, or the machine itself?

The question becomes even more complex when we consider the ethical aspects. Many believe that attributing intellectual property to a machine would be an excessive step that could encourage commodification of art and culture. Others raise concerns about how AI could be used to plagiarize or duplicate existing works of art, diluting the uniqueness and intrinsic value of human creativity. In the face of these considerations, it becomes clear that current laws are inadequate to address the challenges posed by creative AI.

But it is not only intellectual property issues that give us pause; there are also ethical implications related to responsibility and accountability. Suppose a creative algorithm generates content that is offensive or even illegal. Who gets the blame? Is it ethical to use creative AI in fields such as journalism or medicine, where accuracy and integrity of information are paramount? What about using AI to create deepfakes, which can manipulate the perception of reality and have serious social and political repercussions?

It is critical that practitioners, ethicists, and legislators work together to navigate this rapidly changing environment. New laws and regulations, or at least an adaptation of existing laws, may be needed to ensure that creative AI can thrive without compromising the ethical and legal principles we value. At the same time, we must be open to dialogue and reflection, inviting diverse voices into the debate about how AI can influence the future of human creativity.

Addressing the ethical and legal challenges of creative AI is not just a matter of regulatory adaptation, but also of collective introspection. It is an opportunity to reconsider what it means to be creative and what values we want to preserve in a world increasingly influenced by technology. AI forces us to face issues that go to the heart of the human condition, prompting us to reflect on what we really want from this extraordinary marriage of man and machine.

In today's digital landscape, creativity is no longer the exclusive domain of humans. Artificial intelligence (AI) is channeling its potential in ways that challenge the conventional limits of human ingenuity. It is now capable of composing music, generating images and writing text that could fool even the most experienced observer. Yet beneath this brilliant layer of innovation, ethical issues emerge that deserve deep scrutiny.

Imagine an AI algorithm creating a musical composition. The composition is indistinguishable from that of a human being and touches the strings of emotion and intellect in a masterful way. But to whom does this piece belong? Can AI claim copyright? And, in a broader context, its ability to create art raises concerns about originality and authenticity. If art is an extension of the human experience, what does it mean when a machine can replicate it so faithfully?

Then there are the ethical issues related to responsibility. When an algorithm creates something controversial or potentially harmful, who is responsible? Is it the programmer who coded the algorithms? Is it the user who set the parameters? Or is it the broader society that allowed such technologies to develop without a proper ethical framework? The question of accountability is a tangled thicket of legal and moral complications.

One of the most sensitive aspects of ethical challenges is social justice. AI algorithms are trained on data that, more often than one might think, reflect existing biases and inequalities in society. So when AI creates something, there is always the risk that it will perpetuate harmful stereotypes and inequities. In a world where art and culture are powerful means of representation, the impacts of this ethical challenge are profound and enduring.

And then there is the concern about cultural identity. AI can easily appropriate elements from various cultures to create something "new," but this raises questions about cultural heritage protection and cultural appropriation. In an era when technology can easily access global resources, it is critical to ponder how to preserve the integrity of cultures.

Looking ahead, it is clear that the ethical challenges of creative AI will certainly not dissipate. In fact, they are likely to become increasingly complex as technology advances. The implications are immense, not only for artists and creators, but for society as a whole. It will therefore be critical to develop a robust and inclusive ethical framework that can guide the evolution of creative AI.

One way to do this might be to engage a broader range of voices in the dialogue on these issues, from the scientific community to policymakers, from artists to ethicists. Another avenue might be the implementation of ethical audits during the development and deployment phases of creative AI technologies.

So while we marvel at the feats of AI in the creative field, it is crucial to remember that with great power also comes great responsibility. It is a responsibility we all must share if we are to successfully navigate the increasingly complex future of creative AI.

CHAPTER 10: BEYOND TODAY: THE FUTURE OF CREATIVE AI

Navigating the vastness of the field of artificial intelligence, it is easy to feel overwhelmed by the sheer volume of technological innovations. But today I offer an alternative track, away from the complications of tensors and the challenges of algorithms. Let's take a journey into the world of tomorrow, where artificial intelligence will not just be a tool, but a creative partner, a digital muse that might even give new meaning to the phrase "human invention."

Imagine a world in which artificial intelligence goes beyond its traditional function as an assistant or facilitator to become an active collaborator in the realm of creativity. We are already seeing the first steps of this phenomenon in areas such as art and music, where generative algorithms work together with painters and musicians to create new and innovative works. But what if we extend this concept to less conventional areas, such as creative writing, music composition or even philosophy?

One of the most challenging concepts is that of artificial intelligence as a kind of "creative platform," a canvas on which humans can paint their ideas in a deeper and more meaningful way. Take for example the concept of "ethical AI," a subdiscipline that explores how artificial intelligence systems can make ethical decisions. In the future, we may see algorithms that not only help ethicists model the most complex topics, but also autonomously generate new ethical theories or concepts for further human reflection and debate.

But even in the everyday, creative AI has the potential to revolutionize the way we live and work. Think of applications in interior design, where AI could work with architects and designers to create spaces that are not only aesthetically pleasing, but optimized for psychological well-being. Or consider the potential in fashion, where algorithms could design clothes that change color or shape based on your mood, thanks to embedded biofeedback sensors.

One of the biggest obstacles to realizing this future is the question of the "personality" of AI. If we want AI to be a creative collaborator, it is crucial that these machines have a sense of individuality. Recent work in the field of "AI personalization" is exploring ways to create systems that can adapt to users' tastes, preferences, and even moods, making interaction with AI more natural and intuitive.

The road to creative AI is strewn with unanswered questions and ethical dilemmas. We will face challenges such as intellectual property, copyrights, and even the social and cultural implications of shared creativity between humans and machines. But despite these uncertainties, it is impossible not to feel thrilled at the idea of what the future might bring.

So let us look beyond the horizon of today to a world in which artificial intelligence is not just a calculating entity, but a partner in exploring the infinite possibilities of human thought and creativity. In this new world, we will not only learn from AI, but we will expect it to learn from us, growing into an ecosystem of innovation and discovery that will benefit all aspects of society.

The future of Creative Artificial Intelligence (AI) is taking shape before our eyes, in a dynamic synergy of engineering, ethics, art, and bold visions of tomorrow. We often think of AI as a purely analytical force, optimized to process data or solve complex equations. But there is unexplored territory where AI marries with human creativity, and that is where a revolution is happening.

Imagine a world where AIs assist composers in writing symphonies that challenge the conventional boundaries of music theory. Think of a museum where paintings are designed by algorithms capable of understanding and emulating artistic styles ranging from the Renaissance to Impressionism and beyond. This is not just the grain of a utopian vision; it is a realistic possibility fueled by the current frontiers of research.

From academic labs to start-up garages, efforts are underway to teach machines not only to think, but also to "feel" in the most artistic sense of the word. One of the most promising tools in this context is the Generative Adversarial Network (GAN), a class of machine learning algorithms. GANs are proving that they can produce visual art, compose music and even write poetry in styles that are indistinguishable from human styles. In some cases, works created by GANs have already won recognition and awards.

But what will be the impact of these innovations on our concept of creativity and, more generally, on human culture? On the one hand, there is the potential for an unprecedented democratization of art and design. AI could make artistic disciplines more accessible, breaking down the economic and technical barriers that today limit access to the means of creative production.

On the other hand, complex ethical issues emerge. Who owns the copyright in an algorithmically generated work of art? And what value should we place on "authentic" art in an age when machines can emulate styles with impressive accuracy? These are questions that force us to ponder the very meaning of creativity.

And as we navigate these uncharted waters, it is crucial not to lose sight of the social and political implications. Creative AI could amplify or even radicalize existing dynamics of power and control. It could be used to manipulate public opinion through the generation of false but credible news or to reinforce harmful stereotypes through artistic representation.

Research on these and related issues is more relevant than ever. We are just at the beginning of a new era in which AI and creativity coexist and interact in ways we could only have imagined a decade ago. And as we venture beyond today, it is our job as engineers, artists, ethicists, and citizens to shape this future in responsible and enlightening ways.

The idea of artificial intelligence (AI) as an advanced computational tool is outdated; we are now exploring the dimension of creativity. Imagine a world where AI is not just an assistant, but an artistic collaborator, an educational mentor, and even a philosopher. This is the direction in which we are moving, and it is a journey that promises to be as compelling as it is innovative.

In the field of creativity, AI is already contributing in ways that were once unthinkable. From music generation programs to graphic design systems, the machine is learning not only to replicate artistic patterns but also to come up with new art forms. Think of software that can create paintings in styles ranging from Renaissance to abstract, or algorithms that can write original poetry. What makes these possibilities particularly exciting is that AI can become an amplifier of our creative abilities, offering unexpected perspectives and allowing us to explore artistic domains that were previously inaccessible to most people.

And it's not just about art. Science, philosophy and even spirituality could be fertile grounds for creative AI. The implications for training and education are immense. Imagine a learning environment in which each student has access to a personalized AI mentor who can adapt the curriculum in real time to maximize individual potential. This would not only make education more accessible, but also more personalized. AI could play the role of an additional educator, able to identify gaps in the learning process and provide specific solutions.

However, we must also consider the possible pitfalls. The ethical question is unavoidable: how will we ensure that AI is used responsibly, especially in such personal areas as education or the arts? We will need to develop rigorous ethical standards and regulations governing the use of AI in these domains, because the potential repercussions of wrong implementation can be severe.

Another key consideration is the relationship between man and machine. While AI could free educators from mechanical tasks, providing them with more time to focus on more human aspects of teaching, we must also be aware of the possibility of overdependence on technology. The goal should be a balance in which AI is a complement, not a substitute, for human interactions.

We are at the dawn of an era in which creative AI could radically transform our understanding of training, education, and even what it means to be human. As we venture into this new territory, it is critical to be aware of both the extraordinary opportunities and the ethical and societal challenges involved. Developers, educators, artists, and all of us have a role to play in shaping this future. It is a task that goes beyond today, extending into a tomorrow that could be both amazing and profoundly meaningful.

In today's digital landscape, artificial intelligence has permeated almost every aspect of our daily lives, from facial recognition to virtual assistants. But as the technology advances by leaps and bounds, a fundamental question emerges: what will be the future of AI in the creative realm, and how can we make it sustainable?

It is no secret that artificial intelligence has already demonstrated that it can emulate, to a certain extent, human ingenuity in areas such as music, visual art and writing. But is this really creativity, or is it just advanced imitation? The answer to this question may be the key to understanding the future of AI-generated creativity. More importantly, it will help us understand whether these innovations can coexist sustainably with human and environmental well-being.

Creativity is commonly understood as an inherently human activity, a process involving not only technical skills but also empathy, intuition and cultural context. But if we see AI as a powerful tool that can extend and amplify human creativity, rather than replace it, then we begin to glimpse the endless possibilities that could emerge from this symbiosis.

Another critical aspect to consider is the environmental impact of the growing reliance on AI systems for creative purposes. The large data centers that power neural networks consume enormous amounts of energy, often generated from nonrenewable sources. Therefore, if we are to chart a sustainable future for creative AI, we must be prepared to balance technological innovation with a strong commitment to environmental sustainability.

There are already initiatives that seek to mitigate the ecological impact of AI technologies, such as adopting renewable energy to power data centers or developing more energy-efficient algorithms. But there is still much to be done. We should also question the very meaning of 'sustainability' in this context. It goes beyond mere environmental compliance and also embraces issues of ethics, equity and inclusiveness.

Artificial intelligence has the potential to democratize access to creativity, allowing anyone to express themselves in ways previously unthinkable. However, there is a risk that this democratization could become a further polarizing force, in which people with access to advanced technologies have an undue advantage over those less fortunate.

Let us imagine a future in which artificial intelligence is not just a tool in the hands of human beings, but a partner, an extender of our creative abilities. We imagine a future in which the energy needed to power these magnificent machines comes from sustainable and renewable sources. Let us imagine a future in which creative opportunities are more equally distributed, regardless of each individual's socio-economic background. Only then can we say we have found a balance, a point where technology and humanity, innovation and sustainability, coexist in a harmonious and fruitful ecosystem.

Answering these questions and addressing these challenges is not just a task for scientists, technologists or artists, but for all of us. Each of us has a role to play in shaping this uncertain but exciting future. Creative AI is a frontier we are just beginning to explore, and as with any new frontier, caution is as necessary as boldness. But one thing is certain: the journey will be as extraordinary as the destinations we reach.

The artificial intelligence landscape is evolving at a staggering pace, creating unprecedented opportunities and challenges. One of the most exciting and controversial areas is undoubtedly Creative AI, an area that sees machines trying their hand at tasks traditionally considered the preserve of human intelligence, such as art, writing and music composition. But what does the future hold in this rapidly developing domain?

For many, Creative AI represents an ethical dilemma. On the one hand, there is the prospect that artificial intelligence could free humans from monotonous tasks, allowing a greater emphasis on innovation and discovery. On the other hand, thorny issues arise regarding intellectual property, authenticity and the value of human contribution. For example, if an algorithm composes a symphony or writes a novel, who gets the credit? And what is the meaning of "creativity" in a context where a machine can generate works of art at a speed unimaginable for a human being?

One of the most intriguing aspects is the potential collaboration between artificial and human intelligences in the creative process.

Already we are seeing an increase in platforms that facilitate this synergy, allowing artists, writers and musicians to use AI as a tool to expand their repertoire of expression. But as machines become increasingly competent, there is also growing concern that they may begin to replace humans in roles that require emotional sensitivity and interpretation. The challenge, then, is to balance the use of AI as an empowering tool without distorting the essence of human art and creativity.

Nor can we ignore the economic implications. With AI producing content at an exponential rate, the market could be flooded with algorithmically generated "creative" works, reducing the perceived value of human labor. This could lead to a reorganization of the economics of creativity, with new remuneration models and greater emphasis on other elements, such as interpretation or curating. In addition, new questions are emerging about copyright-related jurisprudence. How do we regulate works created by algorithms? This is still unexplored ground that needs an open and inclusive debate.

What about the potential of technology in bringing forth new forms of art and expression that might not be conceivable through human ingenuity alone? Think of hypercomplex architectural structures or new genres of music that might emerge from human-machine collaboration. At the same time, there is a risk that Creative AI could standardize aesthetics and stifle cultural diversity. After all, algorithms are trained on existing data and can therefore perpetuate and amplify cultural trends and biases.

The road ahead is thus fraught with uncertainties, but also with immense possibilities. Creative AI could represent a new frontier in the history of human creativity, but it is essential that we approach this future with open eyes, open hearts, and open minds. The discussion about the role of AI in the creative world is as urgent as it is inevitable, and each of us has a place in the dialogue that will shape its impact on our future.

EPILOGUE

Imagine a world where a computer can write a symphony that makes you cry, a digital sculpture that leaves you breathless, or a novel that keeps you glued to the last page. "The Art of AI: How Technology Affects Creativity" is a groundbreaking guide that unveils the veil on this exciting new frontier where art and technology dance in an intricate tango of possibilities.

In the first chapter, we explored how artificial intelligence is no longer just a set of algorithms and calculations, but has become a collaborative partner in the creative ecosystem. We traveled through time, from the earliest artistic explorations with AI to the current dizzying advances, and probed both the turbulent waters of ethics and the vast depths of unexplored potential.

The book subsequently delved into the technical underpinnings that power these wonders. You discovered how generative algorithms, neural networks and new software are changing the face of creativity, from music to fashion. Whether you are an artist, a programmer, or simply an inquisitive enthusiast, these concepts serve as a foundation for understanding the practical applications that follow.

And what better representation of the potential of this fusion of man and machine than music? We examined how AI can help in the composition, arrangement, and even analysis of music, paving the way for new genres and sound experiences. From Bach to the Beatles, imagine what might emerge from this new symbiotic relationship between musicians and machines.

But it is not only music that is being revolutionized. Visual art, literature, and film are just as many theaters in which AI is offering new ways to express human vision. Have you ever thought about how an algorithm could help restore a Renaissance masterpiece? Or how it might interpret and bring to life the characters in a novel? These are no longer rhetorical questions; they are today's reality.

Nor should we forget fashion and user experience design, where AI is creating sustainable, personalized solutions. From tailored suits to interfaces that adapt to user behavior, AI is becoming a highly competent stylist and designer.

However, like any new frontier, creative AI presents its own ethical challenges. From copyright issues to concerns about employment and discrimination, it is crucial to think about social responsibility as we venture into this new territory.

This fascinating journey concludes with a look into the future, the limits of research, and the impact on education and training. How will the creative landscape change in the coming years? Only time will tell, but one thing is certain: AI is here to stay and the dialogue between human creativity and technology has just begun.

We are pleased to have shared this journey with you, providing you with the tools to explore, understand, and hopefully contribute to this exciting evolution. With "The Art of AI," you now have a map for navigating the intersection of art and science, a guide to actively participate in the debate that will shape our creative future.

Stay curious, stay creative, and most importantly, stay open to the endless possibilities that emerge when humanity and technology join forces in a magnificent ballet of innovation.

ABOUT THE AUTHOR

Harry J. Smith

Harry J. Smith is an eminent figure on the artificial intelligence scene, but not in a traditional way. His distinctiveness lies in his distinctive multidisciplinary approach that blends technology, philosophy, and art into a refined amalgam of knowledge and insight. With a degree in Computer Engineering from a prestigious university and a doctorate in Philosophy of Science, Harry has always exhibited an insatiable thirst for knowledge that transcends academic boundaries and siloed specializations.

Despite his solid academic credentials, Harry is not an abstract theorist. He has collaborated with innovative start-ups, leading academic institutions, and industrial giants in the field of AI, putting his sophisticated theories into practice. His career path is studded with prominent positions as a consultant, researcher, and lecturer. His authority in the field is recognized by both industry and the academic community, a testament to a multifaceted career and the ability to combine practice and theory effectively.

His book, "The Art of AI: How Technology Affects Creativity," is a fascinating journey through the intersections of artificial intelligence and the humanities. With fluid and accessible writing, Harry explores how AI is transforming not only the way we live and work, but also the way we express our creativity. It is a text that captures the reader's imagination, forcing them to question fundamental questions such as the essence of creativity, the importance of ethics in AI, and the role of technology in the evolution of society.

In addition to being an acclaimed author, Harry is also a much sought-after speaker. With his magnetic eloquence, he has a gift for making complex topics accessible to a wide audience. His lectures, seminars and workshops are a combination of scientific rigor and provocative insights, often peppered with personal anecdotes that make his passion for the subject tangible. He is one of those rare individuals who can speak with equal ease about complex algorithms and aesthetic theories, building bridges between worlds that often seem irreconcilable.

But what really sets Harry apart is his humanity. Despite his formidable intellect and impressive accomplishments, he remains an incredibly approachable and friendly person. He is known for his ability to listen and the empathy he shows toward others, qualities that shine through both in his writings and personal interactions. For him, artificial intelligence is not just a field of research or a set of problems to be solved; it is a lens through which to explore the very essence of the human experience.

The depth and scope of his work make Harry J. Smith a unique authority in the field of artificial intelligence. His book "The Art of AI" is a must-read for anyone interested in understanding how the advent of AI is redefining the contours of human creativity and technological possibilities. With his talent for communicating complex ideas clearly and engagingly, Harry is not only an expert in his field, but also a bridge between different worlds, a catalyst for dialogue and understanding in an era of rapid change and uncertainty.

www.ingramcontent.com/pod-product-compliance
Lightning Source LLC
Chambersburg PA
CBHW071303050326
40690CB00011B/2513